Masterfoods is the power b‹
Incorporated in Europe. Ou‹
Mars® Twix® Whiskas® & Pe‹
world's largest privately ow‹
turnover exceeding 14 billio‹

CW01064154

Mike Oldridge
Age: 24
Degree: (M Eng.) Mechanical Engineering
   - Durham University
Joined Masterfoods, part of Mars, Incorporated: 2000
Current Role: Project Engineering

There were several aspects that attracted me to Masterfoods, part
of Mars Incorporated. The reputation of a large well respected
company, the way Masterfoods looks after their associates and the
friendliness and openness of all the people I had met. It is a very
lively and dynamic place I knew that I would enjoy working here.
I spent the first of my three placements at the Melton site working
in reliability. This involved increasing the efficiencies of the existing
petfood canning lines and implementing more cost effective
maintenance strategies.

My second placement was in King's Lynn working on the Dolmio,
and Uncle Ben's pouch lines. This was a combination of managing
the design, installation and commissioning of new equipment and
also being responsible for increasing pouch capacity.

My third and final placement is back at Melton in the projects
team, working on the design of a new multi-variety multi-pack
canning line and heading up a team to install print and apply
machines on all packaging lines to reduce costs and improve
traceability of product.

Ideally I would like to remain in Projects after the end of my
training programme to achieve chartered status. My other goals
include obtaining cross-functional experience working in other
roles such as Operations or Commercial not just in the UK but also
abroad.

Mike is currently completing his Engineer Development
Programme, one of the graduate development opportunities
offered by Masterfoods.

WHAT NEXT after university?

LAWYERS AT THE HEART OF GOVERNMENT

The Government Legal Service (GLS) employs around 1760 barristers and solicitors across 40 government organisations. Our lawyers are involved in every aspect of government. So they deal with issues from agriculture to architecture, energy to employment and immigration to industry. We offer unrivalled access to the issues facing government, unique intellectual challenges and an amazing opportunity to develop careers across a diverse portfolio of work and the GLS.

For information on opportunities at all levels - including vacation placements, trainee solicitor and pupillage opportunities, and qualified entry please go to www.gls.gov.uk

THE TIMES

WHAT NEXT after university?

WORK * TRAVEL * EDUCATION & LIFE WITH A DEGREE

SIMON KENT

KOGAN
PAGE

First published in Great Britain in 2003

Kogan Page Limited
120 Pentonville Road
London N1 9JN
United Kingdom
www.kogan-page.co.uk

British Library Cataloguing in Publication Data

A CIP record for this book is available from the British Library.

ISBN 0 7494 3974 2

Typeset by Jean Cussons Typesetting, Diss, Norfolk
Printed and bound in Great Britain by Cambrian Printers Ltd, Aberystwyth

Get the taste for these opportunities?

Food is one of the fastest moving consumer issues in the UK. BSE, GM foods, food labelling and organic foods are just some of the recent headline stories. The Food Standards Agency is at the forefront of protecting public health.

Our aims

- Provide advice to the public and to the Government on food safety, nutrition and diet.
- Protect consumers through effective enforcement and monitoring.
- Support consumer choice through accurate and meaningful labelling.

An independent voice acting in the public interest, our UK headquarters are based in London, with offices in Scotland, Wales and Northern Ireland and we employ around 550 staff. The Meat Hygiene Service - which also has the protection of the public as a primary aim - is accountable to the Agency and employs a further 1500 staff.

Opportunities to suit your skills

We advertise for a variety of exciting roles in a range of different areas throughout the year, including:

Food Science • Nutrition • Microbiology • Novel Foods Veterinary Science • Toxicology • Research Management Project Management • Administration • Policy Making Finance • Information Technology • Communications Legal Services • Human Resources

Scientific roles are our **main area** of graduate recruitment. Involved in scientific policy development and implementation in support of the Agency's key objectives, the roles include collating and interpretation of scientific information, assisting in the management of research and/or surveillance projects, maintenance of scientific databases, as well as provision of advice and producing written briefings.

Our development depends on yours

We are committed to helping you to make the most of your particular talents and ensuring that you can build on your existing skills, as well as providing the opportunity to develop further. You can undertake training to ensure you meet the needs of the job and also some for your own personal development. This includes formal courses in addition to on-the-job training.

Benefits you can enjoy

In return, we offer an attractive benefits package including a competitive starting salary, 30 days paid leave per year, 10$^1/_2$ days public and privilege holidays, flexible working patterns, a choice of final salary pension or stakeholder pension, childcare vouchers and corporate gym membership.

For further details on current opportunities or information about the Food Standards Agency log on to www.food.gov.uk

The Food Standards Agency is an equal opportunities employer and we are committed to recruit a more diverse workforce that reflects the people we serve. We operate a Guaranteed Interview Scheme for people with disabilities who meet the minimum published criteria.

FOOD
STANDARDS
AGENCY

Putting the consumer first

A career in logistics and transport

Where would we all be without logistics and transport? If you thought a career in logistics and transport to be only for a technical egghead with an engineering degree, then think again! We spoke to Dorothea de Carvalho, Director of Professional Development at The Institute of Logistics and Transport, about working within these vital, exciting and rewarding areas of the economy and making a real difference to the way that we live our lives.

What is the relevance and role of logistics and transport in our everyday lives?

Nearly everything we eat, drink, wear or use spends at least some of its time in a warehouse or on a lorry, boat, plane or train. As well as goods, people have to get from A to B as well. Transport planners influence the way we travel and most of us at some point use some form of public transport whether for travelling to school or work or going on holiday. However, without specific people delivering these vital services the whole supply-chain and transport infrastructure would grind to a halt.

What career opportunities are there in logistics and transport?

A career in logistics and transport has something to offer for everyone – right now. This is a great time to enter the profession with good people in demand across many sectors of the logistics and transport profession.

Do I need a degree for a career in logistics and transport, if so what degree disciplines do employers recruit from?

A degree is not essential – however, recruiters will often focus on core subjects, which means that those graduates in subjects that build up good analytical, numerical and management skills may be considered more suitable. Many recruiters do not have any specific requirements – focussing instead on other aspects of a course such as geography, marketing or IT – depending on the role they are looking to fill.

Are there management prospects in logistics and transport and how do I go about getting into this?

There are plenty of management opportunities. Most people looking at the profession with no inside knowledge would probably think it begins and ends with drivers – whether of lorries or buses or trains. However, someone needs to manage those drivers, someone needs to plan the most cost effective routes and what loads are being taken, where and when. Someone needs to plan the timetables to ensure that there is enough drivers and capacity to provide the services as advertised. These activities all require managers to lead and motivate teams and deliver results.

Why should I consider logistics and transport management?

Of course, I may be accused of being biased but ... I believe that logistics and transport management is a great career option and is one that utilises a range of skills. It is ideal for those people who don't want to be stuck in an office all day who don't want the monotony of a dull mundane job and who crave responsibility and variety and maybe a chance to see a bit of the UK or even the world. The salaries compare very favourably with other professions and you have a real chance to make a difference to the way people live and work.

Where can I find out more information about companies that employ people within these professions?

A first port of call should always be your careers service. Ask friends and family for help and information and carefully search through the vast amount of information available on the internet. You should also consider joining the professional body that covers the sector and maximise that investment to the full by utilising the resources and knowledge available throughout your career.

For further information call
The Institute of Logistics and Transport (ILT),
Tel: +44 (0)1536 740104 or visit the
ILT Web site: www.iolt.org.uk

The Institute of
Logistics and Transport

Contents

Get yourself a postgraduate
qualification and a career for life

The creation of new roles and responsibilities means there's never been a more exciting time to become a nurse - roles such as nurse consultant and nurse prescriber, where you are given real responsibility for the care and well-being of patients.

To put you on the right track from day one, the University of Southampton School of Nursing and Midwifery offers a Postgraduate Diploma in Adult, Child or Mental Health Nursing for graduates of a health or social care degree programme (min 2:2).

This challenging two-year programme offers an 'accelerated' route to Registered Nurse status and will enable you to become a highly competent, knowledgeable and skilful practitioner.

For more information visit our website www.nursingandmidwifery.soton.ac.uk or call us on 023 8059 5500.

University of Southampton

school of nursing and midwifery

The University of Southampton is an equal opportunities employer.

Katherine Hunt
2nd year Bachelor of Nursing (Hons)
University of Southampton

I have always wanted to study nursing and had worked as an Auxiliary before I started the course so I had a good idea of what being a nurse entails. Nursing is a great profession to enter, especially now, as there are many new opportunities and extended roles developing. It also provides you with a world-recognised skill, which gives you plenty of scope for travel.

I chose Southampton partly because of the good reputation of the University but also because of the strong emphasis on clinical practice, as I wanted as much clinical experience as possible. We have regular sessions in the skills labs, which I find to be particularly useful as they help to boost clinical confidence and it gives you a chance to practice your skills with course mates.

The University also runs an inter-professional education programme which gives valuable insights into the work of other health professionals and provides an opportunity to meet other students in the Faculty.

The course is busy and involves shift work but there is still time to join clubs and societies, and I have been studying Dutch in the evenings.

When I graduate I would like to work in health promotion and education, but with all the possibilities available I may change my mind!

WORK ME TO THE BONE PAY ME A PITTANCE NEVER GIVE ME A BREAK

....WHO NEEDS A UNION?

FACT: The average trade union member in the UK gets 29 days annual leave, compared with 23 days for non-union members. They also earn on average, up to 8% more.

You're better off in a union...

UNISON is Britain's largest trade union, representing over 1.3 million members working in public services.

If you would like to join **UNISON** or know more call **UNISONdirect** on: **0845 355 0845** or log onto **UNISON's** website: **www.unison.org.uk**

UNISON
the public service union

Part One

A time of opportunity

1 Overview

Congratulations! You have successfully made it through the wonderful world of higher education – or if your journey is over apart from the final exams, there is light at the end of the tunnel. A few years ago you were slaving over your A levels, wondering what university or college life held in store for you. Would you get the right grades to gain entrance to the course you wanted to do? Where would you go to continue your studies? Who would you meet at university? What would you learn and what kind of an influence would your experience have on the rest of your life?

When you went to university you may have had a clear idea of what you wanted to do after getting your qualification. Your degree course may have been vocational with a set career path attached. Having completed that course, however, you may have found that your ideas have changed. You may feel that you need to take time off from any formal education or career activity. You may have been bitten by the travel bug or simply want to try out a few other options before applying yourself to a structured career. Now is a good time to take a step back and get a greater perspective on your life, regardless of which career path you wish to follow.

Alternatively, you may have had only a vague idea of what you wanted to do when you went to university. You knew the kind of work you wanted to be involved in, perhaps the industry sector that interested you, but nothing more definite than that. So what options are open to you now? And what exactly is your new qualification worth in the world outside the education system?

And it is entirely possible that having completed your education you really have no idea what you want to do. You may have chosen your academic subject simply because it seemed an interesting thing to study. You may have had no intention of using the knowledge and skills you've gained vocationally, instead using your university years to gain a qualification at this level and ultimately postponing a decision about what to do next.

Compared to the opportunities that faced you when you finished your A-level education, there are now countless more choices open to you. Obviously you can track down your first job and start working in your chosen industry. With a graduate qualification in your hand, now is the time to go out into the world and see what you can do. Your qualification is a mark of academic achievement which employers recognize and understand. Your degree shows them that you have the determination and discipline to apply yourself to your subject. Depending on the subject, it may also indicate a technical or practical skill. Your degree proves a level of intelligence and no matter what you choose to do in the future, you will always have that marker.

Chances are you've now had around 16 years of full-time education with no time off apart from holidays and maybe one single 'year out'. Apart from those times, the only freedoms you've had in your life may have been limited to research subjects. The only recognition of your achievements thus far may have been favourable comments and marks from your tutors. Now you're in the real world your work can have a real impact on the things around you. You can create your own life and lifestyle – live your life to your priorities. You can choose precisely how you are going to spend your days – working, studying or travelling. And the recognition you get for your efforts may come in the form of a monthly salary, paid leave, bonuses and promotion.

Choosing the way ahead for yourself is a matter of understanding the possibilities, researching the area you wish to be involved in and then dedicating yourself to realizing that goal. This book will give you practical advice on how to move forward. It will give you a clear view of the land in front of you so that you can plan your next step. It will tell you what resources are available to you and how to get the most from those resources – not just your qualifications but also from resources such as any work experience you've undertaken and your personal network of friends and family.

Even if you are certain what your next move will be you need to understand the implications of your choice, realize the possibilities and recognize how best to act upon your desires. You should be aware of other potential employers and what they can offer you and your career rather than accepting an offer from the first company to express an interest in you. If you want to be successful within your first position you need to know how to contribute to the workplace, how to impress without stepping on your fellow employees' toes and how to recognize when you should move on, rather than becoming entrenched in one particular company culture.

If you decide to travel you need to be certain how you will finance this, what you will gain from the experience and what your strategy will be when you return. Your future employer will be impressed by the skills you picked up from organizing and completing a trip around Africa, but will not be interested if you intended to leave the UK, ended up working in a local supermarket, didn't save up enough money for the trip and finally opted for a two-week package tour of Spain.

The most important thing to remember at this point in your life is that nothing is forever. What you do next will have some impact on your career but it is not a one-time forever-binding all-or-nothing can't-go-back decision. Don't be afraid that by taking a job with a large employer you have signed up to that employer for the rest of your life. More importantly, don't believe that the profession and area of your work today will remain constant for the rest of your life. Having completed a long stint of full-time education you have the perfect opportunity to 'dabble' in the rest of the world.

Get the right balance for yourself in terms of pursuing a clear career path and being open to chance opportunities which may arise. Try not to worry too much about the way ahead – there's nothing to stop you from taking a full-time job just to see how it works out. There's nothing to stop you from travelling, away from the considerations of working life, and returning wiser and more employable. There's nothing to stop you remaining in the education system, honing your skills and increasing your knowledge, giving yourself a qualification which sets you apart from the crowd.

Whatever you decide to do, this book is designed to help you. For those seeking their first job, there is practical advice on what to do, where to look, how to apply and how to be the perfect recruit. There is information on all the major sectors where graduates are employed – designed to give a clear image of the workplace whenever you decide to engage with it. If you want to continue in education and training there's information and tips on how to do that too. If you want to travel, this book will put your trip in perspective.

Finally, if you are really stuck as to what to do next this book contains practical advice on how to make that decision. As the options and opportunities for graduates continue to rise and diversify it is easy to become unfocused about the way ahead and to drift aimlessly between activities. This book will help you identify your priorities – to decide what you need to do now in order to get the future you want.

2 Basic options

We can split the basic options for graduates into three broad sections: work, travel and education. While treating these as separate options, they are not mutually exclusive activities. It could be that your first job involves international travel. A Voluntary Service Overseas (VSO) placement, for example, would mean that you would be working full-time in a different part of the world for the next two years. You may want to secure employment with a large company now, but be given deferred entrance in order to spend a year or so travelling. The best of both worlds could be the graduate who secures deferred employment for 18 months and gets a 'golden hello' payment which neatly finances their round-the-world trip.

Whatever you do you will never stop learning. You are certain to need vocational skills in your workplace or problem-solving skills as you circumnavigate the globe. You may be placed on a graduate training scheme which involves management or technical skills-related courses, you may receive in-house or external training and development. Even if you are self-employed you must ensure that you continue to keep your skills and knowledge up to date in order to ensure that you remain employable. In addition to this, practically every professional association in the country now offers its members guidance on 'continuous professional development'. This is an approach to lifelong learning for professionals which ensures that everyone working in a particular area develops and maintains a high level of skills for the work they do.

Work

Many employers look to recruit graduates on an annual basis to bring new skills, talents and a refreshing outlook to their organization.

Large companies and many public sector organizations run graduate induction or training schemes, designed to help their recruits maximize their contribution to their employer as soon as possible. Small and medium-sized enterprises (SMEs) are also a popular destination for new graduates. While these organizations may have fewer resources to support new recruits, the size of the operation means that there are fewer employees, fewer layers of management and therefore a higher level of responsibility for new recruits. A graduate in an SME may find him- or herself dealing with 'live' issues which immediately affect the direction and performance of the operation rather being limited to only one section of a larger organization. The SME recruit may also find greater opportunities for promotion given that there will be fewer people in his or her position.

You should be aware that the competitive nature of business has led to something of a 'war for talent' among the major employers. This war is particularly violent in certain areas of the graduate market where employers are desperate to be regarded as 'the employer of choice' by their employees. With a good degree and clear employment potential, good graduates may find that they are fought over, with golden handshakes, flexible benefits and postponed starting dates being offered left, right and centre.

But while you may find yourself in demand at the recruitment fairs, do not assume that this will set you up for a job for life. The market forces pressing employers to find high flyers who can contribute to their organizations from their first day of employment are the same forces that lead organizations to drop employees at short notice when they can no longer afford to employ them. Economic pressures demand that organizations complete their work cost-effectively and this has meant a near-constant process of 're-engineering' within business or – to put it another way – reorganizing the staff structure so that more work can be completed to a higher standard in a shorter time by fewer people. As a high-flying graduate you may consider yourself fortunate when the reorganization takes place and you keep your job. But you may not consider yourself quite so fortunate later on when you find that you are called upon to work longer hours under increased pressure in order to make up for the workers who have left.

Naturally you can avoid all the hassle and pressure of working for a company by becoming self-employed. You now have the hassle and pressure of finding the work you do as well as actually doing the work itself. Self-employment in one form or another is on the increase as more professionals find that they can secure a better standard of living (factoring in the additional freedom and control they gain over their lives rather than purely from a financial point of view) by offering their skills on a project-by-project basis to a range of employers. Indeed, working this way can be more secure than employment with a single company. Working short-term contracts means that you are unlikely to lose that work once you have won the contract – employers are unlikely to change their minds about your employment or find that the need for your skills suddenly disappears. And since you will have a number of different employers, if one organization goes out of business it doesn't mean that you will be unemployed as well.

Travel

Travel, it is said, broadens the mind. It can also give you an excellent set of skills which employers find attractive. It is not simply the high standard of organizational skills required to arrange and complete an extended trip around the world that interests employers, nor just the international perspective your travels may have given you, but skills such as 'problem-solving' and 'using your own initiative'.

Of course, the fact that employers consider world travel to give you 'problem solving' skills immediately implies that your travel should involve some problems for you to solve. This is not the time to dial up a package holiday operator and book a month in Greece, but to consider buying a Land Rover and running it into the ground across the Gobi Desert – at which point your problem-solving skills really kick in before you die of thirst. This kind of travel has a flavour of the 'grand tour' of medieval times when young people would travel specifically to expose themselves to other cultures, to learn and understand through visiting far-away places. Yes, you can still hang out on Bondi Beach and go scuba diving in South America but don't expect or allow your trip to be considered as just a 'holiday'. Be sure that you recognize and can explain how your experiences contribute to your overall development as a rounded human being and potential employee for when you return.

Gap years are considered to be time well spent by employers – whether you travel round the world, go to one place to work, study and live, or even if you end up taking a year out and staying in the UK to do something you want to do rather than jumping at the first available job. The general view is that such a year gives graduates time to reflect on what they have learnt and what they want to do. The graduate who returns from a trip or a year out and enters the workplace is less likely to be struck by wanderlust and leave before the employer sees some return from their investment in that individual. At the same time, some organizations will happily let their employees take an unpaid 'gap year' during their employment. The idea here is that it is better for the employer that the employee returns in the long run, bringing his or her workplace skills and knowledge back to the company, than that the company has to go through the expense of recruiting and training a replacement.

Education

As mentioned above, it is extremely unlikely that you will completely stop learning or developing your skills once you have entered the workplace. However, while graduate training courses may be structured to complement your first job or provide vocational and professional training, there is always the option of continuing formal education without making a commitment to the workplace.

Having secured a first degree you can go on to earn higher qualifications based on full- or part-time study. These qualifications will usually be structured around personal research projects, and therefore demand more self-discipline from students than is the case for undergraduate studies. To some extent all postgraduate study is vocational – even if there is no clear identified job at the end of it. Further study gives you a specialism in terms of knowledge or skills, and these aspects are highly valued by prospective employers. In other cases, further qualifications may be necessary for your chosen job. You'll need a PGCE if you want to go into teaching, for example. If your first degree was not law based you can take a

Common Professional Exam (CPE qualification) and enter the legal profession.

Further education and research study can lead to a full-blown career in higher education. While you are studying you may be offered teaching work for undergraduate students on subjects you yourself covered a few years previously. This work will be paid and helps to supplement your student finances. This work may grow into becoming a tutor, lecturer and so on. If your studies lead you to turn in a piece of research which makes you an acknowledged leader in your subject, you may find further academic work through publishing and the application of that research. Scientific researchers may even have their work sponsored by large organizations if the organizations feel that their business will directly benefit from the results.

While your enthusiasm may be fuelled by your studies, working within the education sector is much the same as for conventional employers. The education sector has been financially pressed in recent years, and has undergone its fair share of cost cutting and restructuring. Competition for promotion and high-ranking vacancies is just as fierce here as in the private sector.

3 Conventional employment vs. short-term jobs

Of course, you should realize that the length of your employment with an organization will not always be for you to decide. If you are operating in a particularly volatile sector or for a small business – especially for a new start-up – you may find that financial necessity intervenes and terminates your contract before you can get your feet under the desk. There's little you can do about this but you should be able to tell fairly easily if your new job or employer is in a precarious position, and remember that regardless of your talents 'last in – first out' could apply when redundancies are on the cards.

To counter this issue you can take the bull by the horns and decide up front how long your first job should last. You can decide for yourself what kind of position you are looking for at this stage – the level of dedication and commitment you are willing to take on. You might even decide that you quite fancy trying your luck with a struggling start-up firm and work to make that concern a success, even if the odds are against you.

Whatever your decision, you need to recognize that a 'conventional' full-time employment contract which stipulates you will stay with your employer for a number of years, work a certain number of days every year and receive a set level of remuneration requires a different working attitude from a short-term contract which lasts only for the next three to six months – or weeks. It is not a matter of caring less about the short-term job, but about where the job fits into your longer-term plans and where you want your work to lead you.

Do you agree or disagree with one or more of the following statements?

I want to start work but I don't know what my career should be.
I need to make money now. A career can wait.
I don't want to be tied to one employer for the next year.
I can't find an employer I want to work for.
I want to try a number of jobs to see what they're like.

If you agree with any of these statements, you may find short-term work more appropriate for your first position. Remember, taking a short-term contract doesn't mean that you will be any less dedicated to your job. Indeed, many short-term contracts involve a more intensive level of work because of the time scales imposed by your employer. They can be stressful because you are expected to contribute from day one and are less likely to receive the support and induction schemes given to long-term employees. However, this approach does mean that you are not stuck with that single employer and their company for the next 365 days or more. If working life there is hell you don't need to worry too much – you can find something different soon.

These aspects have a lot to do with company culture. Company culture is about how work gets done. Some companies thrive on high pressure and have a culture which consistently pushes employees to perform to the highest standard possible – or else. Some companies encourage competition between employees in the belief that if you are under pressure to outperform someone who wants to outperform you then the organization will benefit. Alternatively, company culture may centre on teamwork. Problems are shared and solved together and individual workers can try new approaches and even make mistakes in order to learn and improve their work.

Any short-term work you get will certainly be essential to the ongoing operation of a company, but you may not see a direct link between your work and the success of the organization. In some instances you may not be able to make the link between your work and what the company does at all, but you will still be expected to perform to your best ability. Short-term work means that you can experience a range of company cultures before determining which one best suits your working style.

Now consider these statements:

I want to contribute to the overall success of my employer.
I need a clear career path through my industry sector.
I want to be able to plan for the next three years.
I want to work for this company.
I want to know how much money I will earn this year.

The conventional employment model gives you much more security. By taking a full-time contract of a year or more you will know how much money you are going to receive, what exactly is expected of you in your current position, how many days' holiday you will have, what your prospects are for future promotion and so on. When you are taken on in this way you will be brought into the company culture – there will be an induction process so that you understand exactly where you fit into the organization and how you can contribute to the organization's success.

If you find an organization whose company culture suits you to a tee you will definitely want to work for them on a long-term basis. Indeed, it may be more damaging for you to accept only a short-term post with such a company, since you will find it frustrating and demoralizing when the contract ends if your employer thinks that you are a short-term worker only and do not want a full-time contract.

The new psychological contract

Whatever your decision, you should remember that few organizations can now offer a 'job for life'. Over the past decade it has been acknowledged that the 'psychological contract' between employer and employee – ie what is expected by each party of the other – has changed radically and irreversibly. There was a time when employees received their monthly pay, were entitled to holiday pay, a sturdy pension plan, regular increases in pay and responsibility, and in return worked the hours required to do the job loyally for their employer. Organizations can no longer promise a job for life. They have reduced the provision of pension plans, removed the certainty of promotion and pay rises. The employer now promises a certain amount of work for a certain amount of reward, but these promises are short term compared with the promises of 20 years ago.

The employees, in turn, now agree to work those hours for that reward, but do not give their unstinting loyalty to the company. If a better offer comes up somewhere else, the employees have the flexibility and ability to drop their current job and take up the other opportunity.

Taken to the extreme, some employees have developed what has been called the 'portfolio career'. Rather than stay in one industry or profession they have moved around, applying their skills and knowledge to a variety of employers and in a variety of ways. With each new employer they have gained new skills, enhanced their reputation and thereby made themselves even more attractive to other employers. Rather than relying on one employer to give them promotion or even new and exciting projects, employees have set out to find such challenges for themselves.

The chances are that over the next 10 years you will work for three or more different employers. You may not do this as a conscious 'portfolio career' and you may never be self-employed. Indeed, so far as you are concerned you may be following an entirely conventional career route since each time you switch employers you are accepting another set of full-time employment terms and conditions. What you must bear in mind – whether you head for short-term work or long-term contracts – is that you have complete control over what you do for a living. Your employer isn't doing you a favour by employing you, they are doing it in order to be successful and make money. Therefore, no matter what your terms and conditions may be, if you become aware of a better opportunity to work which will meet your requirements, you must grasp that opportunity. True, you can temper the move with what loyalty you feel towards the firm – it may be that they can offer you a better deal if you stay on for a few more years – but at the end of the day the workplace moves fast, the competition is tough and you can't afford to let a golden opportunity pass you by.

4 *Planning the next step*

Practically everything in your life changes when you graduate. Your home life changes as your student housemates move on or you move geographically on a national or international basis in order to take your first job. You may lose contact with the friends you made while studying. Naturally you can try to stay in touch with your contemporaries, but there won't be the same daily contact and sometimes the amount of time spent at work can seriously damage the amount of time you spend socializing with anyone.

When you first went to university it is likely that you moved from your parental home to live on or near the university campus. While this may have been debilitating, you were moving to be part of another community – the educational community. You were one of many students – all carrying out similar activities, all faced with the same problems, concerns and anxieties. When you go to work, you will be in a minority within the organization you join. Companies employing large numbers of graduates may keep new recruits together when they first come into the company, and where this is not possible, networking between the new intake is encouraged so that recruits can support each other and share their new experiences. However, such networks may be geographically diverse or range over different functions – so there still may not be anyone else in your position. Having entered the workplace, you may be the only person who has just arrived and doesn't know exactly how and why the company does what it does.

With your education years behind you, if someone sets a piece of work for you to complete there will be more riding on your doing that work well than securing a good grade. Try to postpone a deadline now and you may face serious trouble from your fellow workers and from your boss.

On top of this you need to think about your financial situation. You may be one of the thousands of students who go to their first job with substantial debts, worried about how these will be paid off and wondering whether you will ever make enough money to enjoy life and be financially sound. You may be concerned that if you don't perform well in the workplace your financial situation will simply deteriorate.

The key to managing this upheaval and stress effectively is to make sure that what you are doing is the best option for you at this stage in your life. You need to focus on what you want to achieve (if you have a clear target), whether that goal is in the short, medium or long term. It is easy to get distracted and to compromise the rewards your first job can bring because you're busy trying to deal with one or other of the problems facing you. For example, you may decide that life would be cheaper and easier if you lived with your parents for a while and avoided paying any money for lodgings, but is this really the right thing for you? Are you cutting yourself off from doing other things by living there? Can you get a job you want to do in that area? Will you have the same level of freedom as you would if you were living somewhere else? Are you actually creating more problems – not least by taking up room in your parents' home? Will they be encouraging and sympathetic towards you? Do they understand, appreciate and support what you want to do with your life? Or will they feel that you are avoiding getting on with it?

Making sure of your next move means taking time out to appraise your options, deciding the way ahead and then creating and pursuing a plan that will lead you to that goal. You don't need to know the answer to all life's challenges right now – you don't need to know what kind of house you will buy or how many cars you want to own by the time you're 30. All you need to know is what you want to do next.

If you are still undecided, you can fast-forward to Part 4 of this book which gives some pointers on how to make decisions about your future. But however you choose your immediate goal, once you have a plan for the way ahead you must stick to that plan. Discuss your choices with those around you – taking on board the suggestions of those who have 'been there before' and communicating your ideas to those who need to know what you're doing. But this is your decision and once you have decided the initial actions required you should not let anyone stand in your way.

Be realistic about the next step. You will not be able to do every-thing at once. It is next to impossible to walk out of university into a dream job which gives you everything you've ever wanted and promises to grow and challenge you over the next 10 years. Understand that you can change your mind if the route you take doesn't deliver what it promised at first. But also understand that you should only change your mind and your direction on the basis of experience. You should not abandon your goal of getting a top busi-ness consultancy job because someone tells you that the competition is fierce and it is unlikely that you will get that job. Make your plan, follow it through and revise that plan on the basis of your own expe-rience.

What the plan should cover

1. Your objective: Having achieved my degree I now wish to get a job/get this specific job/go travelling/take another higher educa-tion qualification.
2. Methods: In order to achieve that objective I need to:
   ● find out what jobs are available to me;
   ● apply to that company;
   ● research for my trip;
   ● find out which courses I can take.
3. Other people: List the organizations and people your plan will impact on, people who should be told of your intentions and those who can help you achieve your aims. As you list each one, make sure you know what you need to communicate to each person and think of a basic timetable for when this communica-tion should take place:
   ● future employers;
   ● industry organizations;
   ● recruitment agencies/organizations;
   ● education establishments;
   ● family;
   ● friends.

Half the battle to realizing your goal is getting other people on board to share your ideas. If your family and friends understand and support your decision to go and climb the Himalayas you will find it far easier to pack your bags, buy the ticket and head out there than it would be if you kept this intention a secret. Telling those around you of your intention means that these people will keep nagging you if you don't do it. If your family and friends are set against the idea or don't understand why you want to do it, their objections may help you clarify your motives. Indeed, sometimes the most inspiring and encouraging sound is that of a crowd of sceptics telling you that something is impossible and you'll never do it.

5 *Finding a home*

For most graduates the best option home-wise is to find rented accommodation which is both affordable and practical considering your place of work. If you have been renting as a student, your first home may represent a small step up in terms of standards of living, but don't count on it. Your priorities are affordability and flexibility.

Affordability because you don't want to see your first pay cheque disappear directly into the pocket of your landlord. You may feel that as a hard-working employee you deserve a little luxury, but don't overburden yourself with a long-term rental agreement for a penthouse suite if you don't even know whether the job you've accepted is one you will still want to be doing in a few months' time.

Flexibility because even if you do want to continue doing the job you've landed, there's always the chance that your employer will want to move you on to another geographic location in order to make the most of your skills and for you to get a feel of the entire company. Some large retail companies make a point of moving their graduate recruits every three or four months specifically to give them experience of operations in different locations. You should be clear with your employer from the start how often you will be expected to move and how much help – financially and otherwise – they will give you as you move from location to location.

Ideally, you should find the accommodation after you have found your job. This may seem like extra hassle in the first few weeks of working life, but unless you know where you are working and how much money you can give to a landlord, you may find yourself having to move out of your house a few months into the job.

Be careful who you live with. The people you lived with as a student may not be your ideal housemates now you are at work. It may be fun still to live in the same way, and to hang out with the same people, but unless their lifestyle is changing in the same way as yours, you may find that there are new strains on your relationship. When you start working regular office hours – plus late evenings and any other times your employer expects – you will not think your flat-mate playing records at two in the morning is as big a laugh as you used to. You will find that you need as much sleep as possible to cope with the working days and can no longer merrily stay up into the small hours chatting, drinking or dancing when you are expected to be behind your desk at 9 am the following day. Worse still, as a graduate recruit you may be expected to put in a full day's work and then to go home and study for professional or vocational exams. Again, such study will be impossible if you are distracted by flatmates who still haven't decided what to do with their lives and are instead prolonging their student years, but without observing the study side of the equation.

Depending on your work situation, you may be able to go back to your parents' house to live. If this is the case, give serious considera-tion to all aspects of the arrangement before doing so. You have not lived with your parents for any substantial period of time for a few years. You have changed. They have changed. Your bedroom may have changed – into a spare bedroom or a home office. Your bedroom has changed for a reason. No matter how genuine your parents' joy and pleasure upon seeing you return to their home, sooner or later your presence is going to create problems.

Ask yourself if you can really face going back to the home envi-ronment. Your years of independence mean that no matter what your parents do to make you feel 'at home', it's likely that they will irritate the hell out of you. Before too long your mum will be making you breakfast, expecting you home for tea and making sure you don't stay out too late because you've got work in the morning. You may welcome this kind of attention and find that it helps you adapt to the world of work, but again consider the implications. You may create a workable and mutually beneficial relationship with your parents. You may set down rules as to what they expect from you (money for rent, when you see them etc) and what you expect from them (don't hassle me, respect my freedom, treat me as a lodger etc), but is this preventing you from fully realizing your independent working life?

One of the most common occurrences is that new graduates return home immediately after completing their degree, and then move out again when their job begins and they have secured accommodation relevant for that workplace. When this move is made, parents tend to find that their offspring have left an amount of general 'stuff' behind them. This can lead to even more discord when parents decide to 'rationalize' or 'tidy up' the stuff. If you do end up using a room in your parents' house for storage, make sure your parents realize that this is what you are doing. Let them know what will happen to this stuff and when it will happen.

For some graduates, accommodation is provided with the job. There may be vocational reasons for this – your job requires you to be on site – or practical reasons: it's an international assignment so it is far easier for your employer to point out where you can live than for you to try to find somewhere off your own bat.

Buying a house? Don't. Unless you have a definite job you definitely want to keep doing for an employer who will definitely continue to employ you for the foreseeable future, there is no point. Unless you are financially loaded or can get your parents to come in on the deal, you will have difficulty convincing a mortgage lender to give you the money you need – given that you have no employment record, scant evidence of financial management and no accounts. In any case, the process and hassle of buying property is not something to welcome at this point in your life.

Added to this, it is likely that in order to make the mortgage payments you will need to let a room to someone else, giving you the additional responsibility of being a landlord – responsible for the general upkeep and running of the house as well as ensuring that whoever rents from you doesn't do anything that devalues the property. Buying a home is generally a good financial investment – the value of property is currently rising at a greater rate than any savings account – but in order to get this value back you will need to hold on to the property for a number of years.

Accommodation can be a substantial problem for some graduates later on in their careers. In parts of the country, house prices are so high that it is practically impossible to buy or even rent accommodation on their salary. Public sector workers, including teachers and the police in London and the South East, are experiencing particular difficulties, making recruitment an issue for these organizations. There have been a number of initiatives introduced to try to combat this problem – to give new recruits a way into the housing market – but the tendency is still for new recruits to start their career in these areas before moving to less expensive parts of the UK where their salary will stretch to cover a mortgage. This is bad news for the areas of public sector work affected but as a graduate you may have no other choice.

6 *Organizing personal finances*

Few graduates enter their first job with sound finances. Student loans, bank overdrafts and credit card bills are a fact of life and can add up to one major headache. The key to managing your finances is simple: don't panic. No matter how bad things seem, no matter how much in debt you are and how impossible it is to conceive of a bank account in the black, you are not alone and now that you are working for a living your situation will improve.

As an interesting tangent, research by one financial institution estimated that the average graduate spends £3500 on getting his or her first job. This covers application process costs such as postage and travel as well as clothing. While this may seem a little daunting for you as you look over your debts, it should be remembered that this cost is cumulative rather than something you'll need to find in one go (you've already spent £9.99 of that budget on this book, so it won't hurt that much!).

If your financial situation gives you immediate cause for concern and requires you to address the situation or you'll be out on the streets, this will probably be your primary reason for accepting your first job. If your financial situation is manageable – ie there are overdrafts, credit cards to pay off and a student loan but you can manage the monthly payments and no one is hounding you to pay the full amount back at once – then you simply need to take a realistic approach to your finances and deal with each issue in turn.

Whatever your situation, it is worth remembering two things. Firstly, these financial institutions know that you are a graduate. They designed and provided you with certain banking facilities specifically because you were a student destined to become a qualified member of the workforce. To this extent, the banks have certain expectations of what will happen when you go into the workplace. They have an expectation of how much money you will make and therefore how you will be able to manage your account. The most obvious example of this is the way the Student Loans Company has structured repayments so that you don't start making payments on the loan until the April after you've graduated. Even then the repayment is set at 9% of your income over £10,000. The company doesn't stipulate how long the payback period will be, instead making sure that paying back the money is not going to leave you destitute.

The second point to bear in mind is that at the end of the day you are paying for these financial services. This seems a strange kind of reassurance, but essentially you should always remember that the interest accruing on your overdraft, credit card and loan amount will have to be met by you. This is how the banks make their money – if everyone kept in credit and never spent beyond their means there would hardly be a point to having a banking service at all. As long as the banks can see your account making them money – either through the interest you pay them or through what they can do with the credit balance in your account – they will be happy.

This means that the problems only start when you cannot service the debts you have. This means getting into a situation where you can't make the monthly minimum payments on your credit card, for example, or when your bank feels that you have exceeded your overdraft limit too many times and there seems no evidence of this changing in the future. The ideal situation, therefore, is to impose control over your finances, ensuring that you can meet the demands of your debts while building towards repaying the money you owe.

Cash-flow forecasting

Crucial to this is checking your monthly cash flow. The object of this exercise is to make sure that when you take a job, the amount of money you are paid each month is greater than the amount of money you need to pay out in order to live. The greater the difference between these figures, the easier it will be for you to meet your debt costs and make repayments.

The cash-flow calculation is particularly critical when entering a full-time, long-term job because the last thing you want to do is be locked into earning a set amount of money, only to find that that amount is not sufficient for your needs. For self-employed and short-term workers this is not so much of an issue since you retain the flexibility to go off and find more lucrative work if you discover that's what you need. The worst-case scenario for the full-time, conventional worker would be to be in a position where you are desperate to get out of one job and find a new employer who will pay you more, but find that you are so strapped for cash you have no time or resources to dedicate to that search.

To calculate your cash flow you need to add together all your outgoings and see how this measures up to your monthly income.

Outgoings include:

- rent;
- food;
- services (laundry etc);
- entertainment (films, gigs, pubs, TV licence);
- travel;
- bills (phone, utilities).

If you have difficulty in assessing how much you spend on each of these, keep strict records of all your expenditure over one week, multiply by four and use this as a rough monthly average.

Don't forget to include bank fees/interest on overdraft and interest paid on credit cards. Make sure that you get a clear figure for these two costs. Interest charged on credit cards is particularly expensive so even if you aren't spending more money with the card you will still incur a cost if you don't pay off the entire amount.

If you don't have a job lined up, the outgoings figure will show you how much you need to earn each month from your job. If you know how much money you are going to be paid by your employer you should already see what your financial situation is going to be. Make sure that the figure you use for your income is the net amount your employer will pay into your account – that is, the amount that you actually receive after deductions are made for income tax and other contributions.

Remember that there is a degree of flexibility here: if your calculation doesn't add up – if there's no way you can afford all your outgoings – you can reconsider the amount you pay for accommodation. Alternatively, you may need to reduce your entertainment budget. You need to create a situation where you can start paying back some of the money you owe. You won't be able to pay it all off at once, but if you've done your sums right you will have an idea of how long it might take.

Priority pay

Pay off your most expensive financial service first. If you compare how much interest you are paying on your overdraft to how much interest you pay to the credit card company, you will probably find that the credit card is more expensive. Aim to clear this debt first.

Getting control over your finances can mean opening a new account from which to manage your transactions. Directing your pay packet into a new account means that the money will not be immediately swallowed by any overdraft you have in your current account. It also means that you could get some interest paid on your new account so at least your money is working for you while you decide what to do with it. You'll have to be tactical about this since some banks may start asking difficult questions concerning the whereabouts of your monthly salary if they don't see it in your account with them.

Your cash-flow plan is your guide to your spending. Once you've started earning money you can see where it is going and what you get for your expenditure. You can budget for certain events, and cut back on luxuries in order to pay off more of your overdraft. Divert other funds into a savings account for that holiday, trip round the world or house deposit. With your cash-flow plan you will be able to control your debts in an ongoing situation and keep all your financial service providers happy.

Lucrative ways

If you are highly skilled and heading into business sectors such as accountancy or financial services, you may find that your employer offers you a deal which resolves all your financial problems once and for all. A golden hello is a lump sum – usually thousands of pounds – given to recruits on their acceptance of a job. This can provide an answer to student debt and set graduate recruits on course for a very lucrative career with immediate effect.

There are also training incentives and golden hellos for some teaching positions. These incentives are designed to attract high-performing graduates into the profession. Teaching has long had to compete with more rewarding private sector businesses in getting the talent required to bring on the next generation. While these initiatives do level the playing field between private and public sector remuneration, the nature of teaching means that it is unlikely to persuade those with no passion for teaching that this is the career for them.

A mention of pension

There is something of a pensions crisis in the UK at the moment. With an ageing workforce and under-performing investment plans, there is a substantial shortfall in money available to support workers after retirement. If you start work with a conventional employer you may well be offered access to a pension scheme to which some of your income is paid every month. On the other hand, if you are self-employed, you may consider it worth your while to set up your own pension scheme in order to start saving for the future.

It is not imperative that you join such schemes right now, but in general, the earlier you start saving, the more income you will receive upon retirement and the earlier you could retire. Over the next few years the pensions system is likely to see substantial change in order to make it easier and more attractive for employees to save. Get independent advice before signing away your contributions and understand exactly the possible benefits and risks attached to any scheme.

Part Two

Going to work

7 Culture shock – leaving education and entering the workplace

For everyone, the first experience of full-time professional work is disorientating. Hopefully you will take to your workplace like a duck to water, finding that the atmosphere and support around you help you use your skills and knowledge to the greatest extent possible so that you achieve things of which you never thought yourself capable. On the other hand, you may find the whole experience traumatic.

Whatever the case, you need to be prepared for what is about to happen. Most importantly, you need to quickly understand and adapt to the working culture in which you find yourself. At university you will have had a range of environments in which you could work. You could manage your own study either at home or in the library or even in the café round the corner if you felt that you were most productive there. In the workplace you will find that you have less choice about where you work. You might be in a busy open plan office, able to hear the conversation and work of everyone else. You may have a desk from which you are expected to work for the majority of the day – and if you're not there questions will be asked.

Some employers have wised up to the importance of creating different working environments in order to support high-performing employees. They have set aside more relaxed spaces where people can go to 'chill out' or just hang out with fellow employees away from the pressure of the office. This kind of initiative is not designed purely to give you a space to go to and avoid work, but the hope is that somewhere different will encourage you to feel refreshed, have different ideas and create initiatives that perhaps would not emerge from a round table discussion or arguing across a desk.

Unless you are very lucky you will find that working life takes up far more time than university lectures, seminars and tutorials ever did. As a student you may have enjoyed pursuing further study of your subject in your own time. At work you may be irritated to find that even when you are at home you are still preoccupied with workplace problems. Moreover, these problems can have more to do with 'office politics' than the work you are doing.

Office politics simply refers to the way people get on with each other in the organization. Usually it is to do with gossip around the workplace and the general opinions held by people about senior managers and other members of staff. At its height, office politics may dictate how one is expected to perform in order to succeed. For example, office politics may determine that the only way to gain promotion is to flatter one of the senior managers. Anyone perceived to be doing this might be regarded as a bit of a creep by everyone else.

One area where graduates can experience the negative side of office politics is through the attitude of existing senior managers. Even if you are eased gently into an organization using a tried and tested induction process, sooner or later you are likely to meet someone who's been in the organization for many years, believes he or she knows everything, that graduates know nothing and who wants to know why you have been recruited. Current employees may regard you as a threat no matter how well you fit into the organization or how reliant the organization is on graduate intake. They might believe that you are going to take work away from them or completely change the way they work. You may even experience pressure to perform from the recruitment team or manager who selected you as they want you to prove their recruitment decision right and start making a positive impact on the organization.

If you have been recruited to a management level you may need to organize or delegate responsibility to others who have been in the organization for years. This could be the first time you have ever held such a position of responsibility and you need to be able to make decisions clearly and have the confidence to follow through the decisions you make. There is no easier way to get a reputation as a weak manager than to change your mind about something or directly contradict yourself.

Whether your employer promotes a general feeling of team-work/'we're all in this together' or prefers the 'everyone for them-selves'/'show me the results' culture, if you are working with others your actions will have an impact on their lives. As a graduate recruit you are unlikely to be able to make such a huge mistake that the entire organization goes belly up, but your actions will be scrutinized by the people around you. When you were a student you essentially had only yourself to answer to – the opportunities to study were provided and you had the choice to exploit those resources or to ignore them. Your tutor may have reprimanded you if you were falling behind, but the repercussions were visited on you and you alone. In the workplace, if you are not pulling your weight you will be noticed – by your senior managers and by the people who work alongside and beneath you. They will particularly take note if you are not seen to pull your weight or cause a project to fail or be delivered late.

When you were a student you could select who you wanted to hang out with, who you worked with and so on. At work, it is likely that you will be put together in a team with other people in order to work on a project – and the makeup of that team will be the inspired choice of a senior manager rather than your personal preference. Not only do you need to work with these people but also, as a new employee, you will want to get on well with them and impress your boss. In such situations, being an effective team worker can some-times mean paying more attention to managing your own impact on the team – how you communicate with everyone else, what kind of ideas you contribute and so on – rather than the concerted attention you give to the problem itself.

Many employers will have some kind of arranged social life outside the workplace – anything from a traditional drink in a certain pub at the end of the week, to a full raft of employee benefits such as weekend trips, membership of sports clubs, team sports and so on. Failure to participate in these activities could seriously damage your acceptance in the workplace. Your fellow employees may regard you as someone who just wants to do the job, is no fun and a bit of a stick in the mud. They may like you even less if they find out that having

Become an actuary and combine your problem solving and maths skills with communications and teamwork in an ever-changing financial environment.

Actuaries identify solutions to business problems and manage assets and liabilities by analysing past events, assessing present risks and modelling the future.

Actuaries work in many areas that directly benefit the public through their work in life and non-life insurance, advising pension funds, savings, capital projects, investment, healthcare and risk management. Such work offers management opportunities, with actuaries having a commercial as well as technical role.

Although qualifying as an actuary is a demanding process, the rewards are considerable. An actuarial career offers a challenging, well respected and well paid future. Graduate entry salaries are offered between £18, 000 to £26, 000, and chief actuaries can earn £100, 000+.

To qualify as an actuary, trainees need to be intelligent; most actuaries possess either a first or upper second class numerate degree. The most successful actuaries also have good communication skills. The minimum entrance requirement is grade B at A level or equivalent in maths.

Qualification involves passing the professional examinations of The Faculty and Institute of Actuaries. Trainees take the examinations at their own pace, usually whilst working for an actuarial employer. Exemptions from some of the examinations may be awarded to students who have achieved an appropriate standard in a relevant degree, or have studied actuarial science at postgraduate level.

There are many opportunities for actuaries to use their skills, in the UK and overseas and the demand for actuarial skills continues to grow. The qualification is an excellent base for a business career that is widely recognised throughout the financial world.

To find out more about an actuarial career,
Call 01865 268 228
Email careers@actuaries.org.uk
Or visit www.actuaries.org.uk

The Actuarial Profession
making financial sense of the future

Imagine being able to influence
Government and economies...

Actuaries do every day. By developing a meaningful
picture of the future, based on past and present
information. And that's not all. A qualified actuary is
a problem solver, business analyst, consultant and
financial forecaster. It's challenging work but equally
rewarding - both personally and financially.

To find out more about an actuarial career,
call **01865 268 228,**
email **careers@actuaries.org.uk**
or visit **www.actuaries.org.uk.**

put in a full day's work you socialize exclusively with mates from your old university rather than your new workplace buddies.

The workplace brings with it all these issues and more, which is why it is so important that you identify with your employer's working culture. Going to work brings with it a change in priorities and an extension of responsibilities. Whatever you do, your actions will affect the lives of the people around you. Working life is one of the major ways in which we identify ourselves and relate to each other. The UK population works long hours and spends a significant proportion of its waking life at work. If something goes wrong at work – if the organization we work for hits a bad patch or if we are not happy at work for any reason – it has a significant impact on our life in general. As a student you were responsible only to yourself, but now the stakes are higher. No matter how you feel about your job, you have to take it seriously because your fellow employees take it seriously. They have houses, families, holidays – a complete lifestyle to fund and support – and they will not appreciate it if you regard the company and the work that provides this lifestyle as a joke. Remember, eventually you will gain those responsibilities and will want a sense of security in the workplace in order to give you confidence in your life.

8 *Finding the right employer*

While your job hunt need not be run and managed as a slick campaign, it should certainly not be a haphazard affair. Consider what would happen if you were asked at an interview where else you have been looking for work. Your prospective employer may be a little concerned if you've applied for radically different positions with radically different employers. Certainly you can keep your options open but you are less likely to find an employer if you try to get a position as a business consultant one week and a museum curator the next.

Naturally, were you to be asked at an interview such a direct question as where else have you applied, the correct response is that you have applied and already been seen by your current interviewer's five closest competitors and there's a distinct possibility that they'll all offer you a great starting salary plus benefits. However, creating coherence in your search for an employer is more for your own peace of mind over the next few weeks and months than for anyone else's.

The problem with applying for diverse jobs in multiple industries is that you run the risk of losing all sense of direction. The uncertainty surrounding your future will make it difficult to create other plans or to get a firm grip on other aspects of your life – where you will live, how much rent should you pay and so on. In addition, each time you fill out an application form or go to an interview you have to consciously tailor the presentation of your skills, experience and expectations to match that specific post. If you are applying for one industry or one type of employer then at least you have the opportunity to hone your responses and increase your chances of success over time. If you are applying for different jobs you will have to reinvent your approach each time.

Short-term contracts may not require the same evidence of dedication to specific employers or the same level of industry knowledge. Your employer is not envisaging you stay with the organization for any great length of time, and it is likely that you are being taken on to complete a specific project. Your employer will be less concerned about your general feelings about their company; they just need to be convinced that you can do the work required. Since you won't be in the organization for very long, your employer does not need to ensure that you fit exactly into their workplace.

You will know when you have found your ideal employer because there will be something about the work or the way in which the company operates that really excites you. It will be a business where you feel you can – and want to – contribute almost immediately and which will use and stretch your talents and abilities. It will be an employer who appreciates your skills and rewards them in an appropriate way. The only way you can be sure that the employer you're applying to is this kind of an organization is by undertaking some serious research.

There are many resources for you to use to check up on your employer of choice. To begin with, you may have already identified the best company for you, having had direct contact or experience with them over your student years. There may be an industry-leading organization in your field – a company that consistently innovates and is highly influential within the industry and society in general. They may be obvious market leaders with worldwide operations who employ people with your skills and talents. It may be that you have already seen how they operate through work experience or a placement either as part of a course or prior to becoming a student. You may feel that this organization is the only place to be if you want to be at the top of your industry.

Work experience is easily the best way to suss out whether an employer or indeed an entire industry is for you. Even if you end up doing little more than making the tea for the other employees you will get a good understanding of how that industry and organization operate – a far clearer view than you will ever glean from talking to the people who work there or studying the organization's graduate recruitment literature.

You may find out about your future employer through the media. There may be constant newspaper articles about their operations, TV documentaries on the industry and radio interviews with leading players. You should immerse yourself in the world you want to work in as soon as possible – find out who the important people are, learn the current issues, take on and understand the jargon and technical language used within the industry. This activity works for you in two positive ways: first, you will build up a great understanding of what working in that area means, and secondly, you will make yourself more attractive for future employers.

It's fine to wait for the graduate – and postgraduate – recruitment fairs, but you will have a much better chance if you are proactive, work off your own initiative and approach individual companies yourself. Not only will this make your interaction with the company more personal, but it will flatter potential employers that you find them interesting enough to approach independently. If you can't find any initial contact points through their literature or from their Web site, simply phone up their head office and make enquiries. Do not be daunted by the size or corporate image of an organization. Every company needs to be open to talent and if they're unable to deal with your request for an application form – or can't find the name of someone to whom you can send your white-hot CV – then they clearly don't deserve you.

As you immerse yourself in the culture where you would like to work, you will find that your network of contacts within that sector grows and deepens. You may have casual conversations with other people about the industry in general or about particular firms and thereby discover new projects in which you could play a part. Alternatively, you may find that the same names of high-flying industry professionals keep cropping up. These people may not necessarily be directly involved in recruitment but could still be worth approaching. You can ask their advice on how to get into the industry and ask them how they did it. For small and medium-sized companies (SMEs) you may find it more beneficial to draft a letter of enquiry to a senior or middle manager dealing with the day-to-day operation of the company than to write to a human resources (HR) or personnel manager. Sure, the person you approach may refer you back to the HR or personnel manager, but in doing so will have noted your interest and may even make sure that the person responsible for recruiting chases you up. At the same time, some SMEs are not big enough to have a dedicated HR function, so contacting these people could be your only method of getting noticed.

Today, more than ever before, success in the workplace is as much a question of who you know as what you know. This doesn't mean necessarily that under-talented but well-connected people get the breaks (although it has to be acknowledged that cases exist), but the fact is, with everyone under pressure to succeed and desperate to avoid failure, they are more likely to employ someone they know and have confidence in than someone they've never heard of before.

One of the most neglected and unjustly riled methods of getting the break you need is through using family contacts or your own personal network of friends and associates. You may not be directly related to the managing director of a certain company, but your uncle might have dealt with a few people from that company and therefore have an insight into their business which you otherwise would not have. Your next-door neighbour's brother's cousin might have worked in a similar industry to the one you want to work in, and so on and so forth. This is not a matter of cheating or getting one up on your competitors, it is simply a matter of putting yourself in the best position you can be for getting a job in the area where you want to work.

Concentrating on finding the right employer for you will catalyse your efforts for getting work and offer the coherence you need for your application activities. If you know the kind of people you want to work for, are confident that you can contribute positively, fit into their working culture and will receive suitable reward for your work, you will find that you approach the application process, interviews and 'meet the employers' events with enthusiasm and a proactive frame of mind. Even if you are certain only of the industry and the type of job you want to do, it still means that you can stop worrying about what's going to happen with your life and concentrate on realizing that aim. Ultimately it doesn't matter how you get your first contract with your dream employer; it is your own confidence and enthusiasm that will power you through to a fulfilling position.

Why is now such an exciting time to be a recruitment consultant at PRO?

PRO is an award winning recruitment and human capital management consultancy based in London, Windsor and New York, working with organisations to resource, retain and develop the high performers they need to achieve their strategic objectives. With consistently high year on year growth, PRO is poised to move to the next exciting stage of its development.

We require outstanding individuals committed to achieving at the highest levels with the potential to be the business leaders of the future.

Initially you will join PRO as a researcher, sourcing candidates with a view to becoming a recruitment consultant delivering innovative recruitment solutions to our clients.

To achieve in this role you will need to:

· Be results focused
· Be both able to develop new business and manage existing relationships
· Show an ability to time manage effectively
· Have high levels of credibility
· Have a strong history of delivery

In return you will:

· Be trained throughout your career*
· Work in a professional and high-growth business, one of the 50 fastest growing companies in the UK over the last 5 years**
· Work with London's Young Entrepreneurs of the Year 2002***
· Work in a meritocratic environment
· Have the opportunity to work in the UK and abroad
· Be rewarded in line with your results through salary and bonus package

PRO's exceptional success to date has been due to the drive, passion and ability of our previous graduate entrants, many of who are now in the management team. We are looking for similar people to help us move to the next stage. Send your CV and covering letter stating your reasons for applying to Katherine Ball below.

PRO is an equal opportunities employer
*PRO is accredited as an Investor in People
**The Sunday Times Virgin Fast Track 2001 & 2002
***Ernst & Young's London Young Entrepreneurs of the Year Award 2002

tel: 020 7845 4200   fax: 020 7845 4249
email: careers@pro-rec-org.com web: www.pro-rec-org.com

Marks & Spencer is one of the leading names on the high street.

The UK's largest clothing retailer, we're securing new paths for growth with a sustained expansion in Food, Home and Financial Services business. A Times Top 20 graduate employer, Marks & Spencer's ranking also continues to rise.

The company has evolved to meet the needs of a new generation of shoppers. Unrivalled food development has won back an increasingly discerning customer base. Now we're enhancing efficiency through developing talented and capable people. A determination to dominate every category has led to the advancement of exciting new products, practices and profitability. Now is a perfect time to join a management team that's making room for new ideas.

Developing retail expertise and management skills, Marks & Spencer offers a sought after training ground. Graduates from all disciplines with GCSE Maths and English can apply. The exception is positions in Finance where a minimum of three Cs at A level, or eighteen UCAS points, plus a minimum 2.2 degree is required. A relevant degree is also required for Food and Clothing Technology.

Equally important is evidence of energy, focus, ambition and team spirit. The company's interview and assessment events offer a chance for candidates to demonstrate real passion for retail, ability to manage and engage with people and a common sense approach.

All graduates undertake a formal induction. But nothing beats first-hand store experience of the shop floor. Typically graduates are ready to take on their first management role after 12 months of on-the-job and course based training.

Marks & Spencer offers a valuable lesson in how to be, and stay, successful to those who are genuinely poised to succeed.

Total graduate vacancies: approx 200 Marks & Spencer recruits for opportunities in diverse areas:
Store Management (Selling and HR)
Head Office (Finance, IT, Marketing, Buying)

When to apply: Oct '03-Dec '03

Starting salary: £20,000 plus bonus scheme and location premiums where applicable.

Location of Graduate Jobs:
Store Management: across the UK
Head Office: London

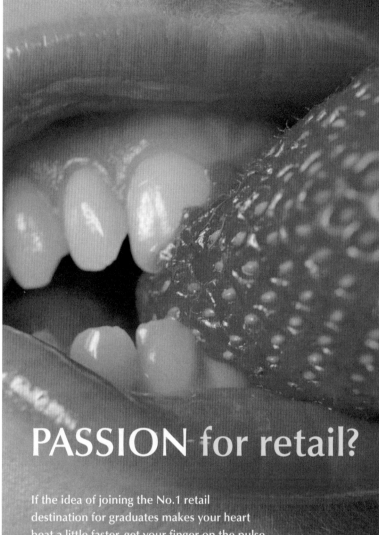

PASSION for retail?

If the idea of joining the No.1 retail
destination for graduates makes your heart
beat a little faster, get your finger on the pulse
at: **www.marksandspencer.com/opportunities**

Marks and Spencer p.l.c is an equal opportunities employer.

**MARKS &
SPENCER**

9 Being the perfect recruit

Your first days at work are likely to be your hardest – not from the workload point of view, but certainly in terms of adapting to your new environment. You will want to impress your employers but will not want to appear as a swot or know-it-all in front of your fellow recruits and work colleagues. You will spend a lot of time getting to know systems and processes and may feel confused and frustrated since these don't appear to make sense or seem to make it impossible for you to do anything practical to help the work of the organization. To cap it all, you will have to observe certain work rules – time and attendance and so on – which can be alien after your recent years of doing what you want to do when you want to do it. At the end of the day, you may be thoroughly demoralized that your first day's experience could be all that faces you for the rest of your life.

The answer to these concerns is to relax. If nothing else, congratulate yourself on the fact that you have overcome one major hurdle and have been given the job in the first place. Remember that your employer clearly sees value in having you on board and therefore it is in their interest to provide you with the opportunities and support through which you can achieve your potential.

Give yourself time to adjust to your new environment and find ways to boost your own confidence within these new surroundings. Dress-wise it is better to overestimate the formality of the workplace. In other words, even if the company has a 'casual' dress code, don't go in with ripped jeans and a baggy sweater. Wear smart clothes so that the people around you will take you seriously and you will make a good impression. There is a chance that you will feel overdressed compared to those around you but you will be forgiven that and can adjust your clothing to a lower standard if necessary. You are less likely to be forgiven if you turn up looking like a student. You will find it harder to win your colleagues' trust and to be taken seriously. You will also reflect badly on the people who have selected you for the organization, and losing their support can be very damaging to your job and career.

Ask questions, listen and understand. Over the first few weeks you are going to be in a position where you are learning things rather than proactively working or creating things. Some graduates may be employed specifically to make a high-level impact on the business, to carry out radical changes or to shake up aspects of the workplace but most will be expected to assimilate the working culture first and make significant contributions or challenges later.

If you have been brought in to make a radical difference, you still need to know how your organization operates. It is impossible to suggest process changes until you understand how things are currently done. It is not just a matter of seeing whether your suggestion is a better solution, but to make a change successful you need to get your communication strategy right. That means understanding where people are now, recognizing their feelings and their reasons for doing things in a certain way and only then working with them in order to make that change. Imposing new ideas out of the blue will not only alienate the people who need to change, but as a new recruit you may immediately create a negative impression of yourself within the company. Your short-term project may fail and you are less likely to be able to make a positive impact in the future.

If you are placed on a structured graduate induction programme, it will be clear what is expected from you, when and where. Such programmes can be strictly timetabled and arranged, but there can still be opportunities for you to exercise your own particular skills and initiative. Very often you will be given a specific project to complete which keys into an aspect of the workplace. In this way your employer gets to introduce you to the working culture while also gaining your ideas of how processes could be improved or changed. It's worth noting, however, that these projects usually result in a presentation to senior managers in the organization rather than you being given the go-ahead to actually make that change.

If a graduate support structure is less tangible, you should seek out the support you need independently. On the one hand this could mean finding other graduate recruits and sharing your experiences of work over the first few weeks. Your fellow recruits may come from your own organization, or they may be within the same industry as you. Even sharing experiences with your old student friends can help provide guidance on how to operate in the workplace. Alternatively, you can look to someone who has been with the organization for a longer period of time, whether they were originally a graduate recruit or not, and use them as a source of information and support – as a guide or mentor for the early period of your employment.

If you do find yourself a mentor, make sure that the person you select has the time and skills to provide the support you need. You are looking for someone with experience of the company and, if possible, the wider industry. You do not want someone who is embroiled in office politics or who will treat you as an acolyte or a menial. Your mentor should be able to offer you sound advice which fits your career and experience, not simply tell you how to get to be in his or her shoes in 10 years' time.

You may not be able to find yourself a mentor within the organization immediately. It can take time to identify the right person, but even on a short-term basis your boss and the others around you who have worked for the organization for a longer period of time will be flattered if you ask them for support or help in finding your place at work.

Some employers like to move new recruits around different functions of the organization, giving them a flavour of each area. This can feel disorientating and make induction a lonely experience, especially if you are being moved around geographically at the same time. In such instances, getting a strong network of colleagues is key to feeling a part of your new organization. If all else fails, you should be able to resource the network through the recruitment function or the training or development department who are charged with guiding you through the induction process. If there appears to be no such network, suggest they make provision for it – you'll impress everyone!

There's only one of you,
do something unique.

Scotland
North East
North West
Midlands
Wales
London
South East
South West

Opportunities
available in
our 28 regional
offices around
the country

We all want to make our mark on life. To prove we've each got something different to offer, something unique. But you can't do that buried inside a faceless organisation as just another number on the payroll.

At Halcrow we feel the same. And taking on individuals like you has allowed us to win an unparalleled variety of impressive projects. It's made us one of the top five consultancies in the UK.

We're an innovative company where individuals work together to creatively solve design, planning and management problems. And make a positive impact on people's lives and their environments.

Offer us a good first/postgraduate degree in a relevant subject and we'll offer you a choice of project opportunities that cover the following disciplines:

Water and Utilities: Irrigation, Drainage, Dams and Hydro, Ports and Dockyards, River Engineering, Water Supply, Waste Water, Coastal, Water Resources, Mechanical, Electrical and Energy, Nuclear and Geomatics, GIS and Special Structures

Transportation: Air Transport Planning, Bridges, Geotechnics, Engineering Geology, Highways and Rail

Property: Building Structures, Building Services, Land Development and Facilities Management

Consulting: Environment and Transport Planning

Check out the graduate opportunities on our website and download an application form. Alternatively, contact Jodie Curtis, quoting reference 1818, Halcrow Group Limited, Burderop Park, Swindon, Wiltshire SN4 0QD. E-mail personnelbp@halcrow.com

INVESTOR IN PEOPLE

For more information and to learn about other opportunities visit:
halcrow.com
Committed to equal opportunities

QinetiQ

QinetiQ is Europe's largest science and technology organisation. A place where the intelligence, imagination and energy of some of the world's leading research scientists combines to make the impossible an everyday commercial reality in all walks of life.

We used to be DERA, the renowned Government R&D agency responsible for the jet engine, thermal imaging and carbon fibre. Now, with the liberty to exploit our capabilities in open markets, we are a world leader in the creation and application of technology.

With over 9,500 people, including Europe's largest community of scientists, engineers and technicians, we have a culture inspired by free thinking and groundbreaking research.

We have the facilities and expertise to tackle complex scientific and technical problems in fields ranging from media to healthcare, aerospace to security, telecoms to transport, defence to finance. So we offer a broad range of careers covering operational analysis, scientific research, development, test and evaluation and project management.

More talent
QinetiQ is a unique organisation seeking around 300 extraordinary new people a year. We look for proactive, analytical, forward-thinking graduates from most science, engineering, IT and numerate disciplines. People with the commercial instinct, questioning mind and passion to plot their own development and take full advantage of our organisation.

More quality
We offer a good salary and benefits package combined with real quality of life – the chance to do interesting work in a pleasant environment with flexible working practices.

More training
From induction through to mentoring and assessment, our integrated graduate development scheme is focused to provide you with the relevant technical and commercial training to help you reach your full potential.

In addition to core graduate development there is the potential to attend international conferences, undertake secondments to customers and, where appropriate, support for further qualifications, such as Chartered status, an MSc, or PhD.

Whether you want to follow a technical path or take a business or project management route, you'll be surrounded by opportunities. But it will be up to you to take them.

More information
For a fuller picture of QinetiQ and to apply online to our all year round recruitment programme, visit www.QinetiQ.com/careers

Name something that's completely impossible.

10 The application process

The way in which you come to the attention of your future employer will vary according to the size of their organization, their recruitment process and the position you hope to take. You may go through every single process listed below, you may only go through one. Whatever happens and whenever it happens, be sure to follow these rules:

1. Always provide the information the employer wants in the way they want it. Employers who ask for application forms only will not read detailed accompanying letters. If you are expected to put all your work experience and qualifications onto the application form, do that and don't put it anywhere else. Similarly, when you're asked a question at interview, answer that question and stop talking when you have finished. Don't talk around the subject or ramble on about something else.
2. Never lie. You might think you're impressing them, but you will be found out. Indeed, you'll probably be found out two weeks into the job when you find that you can't do what's expected of you. This is always embarrassing, but it can sometimes be dangerous as well.
3. Be efficient. Be certain of deadlines, appointments, interview locations and what to wear. Give yourself too much time to prepare for everything.
4. Rehearse, rewrite, rethink. Every time you present something to your future employer, it is with your top performance. The words you write on your application form are words you've slaved over and rewritten five times in order to get the phrasing exactly right. Your interview answers are speeches you've delivered to the mirror, to your friends, tutors, career advisers and even family – improving each answer whenever you've received feedback. As

time goes by and you fill out more forms, send more letters and meet more employers, you will find your skills at identifying how to say what continually improve. This means that even an unsuccessful interview has a positive outcome as it gives you valuable experience.

The application form

This is the most structured method of applying for a job, and you'll find that some organizations have specific forms for specific posts and for specific applicants such as graduates. Read the form at least three times before thinking of picking up your pen. Even then, don't put your pen on the application form itself.

First, make sure that this is the right application form for you. This may seem obvious, but in some cases you may find that the form asks you for evidence of qualifications or work experience that is impossible to get when you're a recent graduate. Check that you have the right form before leaving blank spaces or filling boxes with 'Not applicable'.

Make sure that you understand precisely what is being asked of you and in how much detail. Some application forms will ask for qualifications and experience to be listed in reverse order, some leave it to you to decide the order. There may be separate boxes in which to list your higher education qualifications, your GCSEs and A levels and yet another box for additional qualifications.

Due to high numbers of applications, some organizations have computerized the processing of paper forms. This entails scanning each application form and then using a word or phrase search to separate those who have the desired qualifications or experience from those who do not. If you put your qualifications in the wrong box, therefore, or make a similar mistake, the computer will not identify you as a potential recruit. In addition, it's clear that if nothing else your application form must be easy to read and phrased in a way that highlights the elements you know your employer definitely needs.

Some employers accept – and even expect – applications to be completed online and submitted via the Internet. Again, these forms are designed to take the manual labour and time out of the initial sorting process. The computer will search for specific elements within each application and turn what is usually a large number of average-quality applications into a small number of high-quality applications.

Make sure that your application form sells your skills completely. Your employer may not fully appreciate the skills you have picked up over the years. For example, you could be one of thousands of applicants with your qualification who were also members of the Industrial Society at university, but unless you state that while a member you organized a series of popular and high-profile events, thereby developing organizational and communication skills, your employer will not know that you have these skills.

The application form should provide points of interest for the employer to pick up on. It should not be exhaustive or give the full story of your life. The successful application form will give the employer confidence that this person can do the job, and also offer points of intrigue – aspects of the applicant which it will be interesting to investigate further – how did they manage to get work experience with that company and what specific things did they learn while there that will be beneficial to this business? Get this balance right and not only will you be invited to interview, but you will have a fairly good idea of the kind of things you will be asked about.

Finally, make a copy of every application form you send out. If you do an interview you'll want to know precisely what you have told your interviewers. There may be differences in the way you have expressed your talents between application forms and the last thing you want to do is be tripped up by your own syntax.

The interview

Easily the most daunting part of the application process, this is when you come face to face with your possible employer. They will already know something about you, having read your application form or CV, but now is your chance to impress by being a likeable, exciting, bright young addition to their organization. The key to realizing this is, of course, preparation.

You should already know a lot about the context of this interview: Are you one of many people being interviewed? Are you being interviewed through your own initiative? Do you get the impression that they already want you to do this job and this interview is more of a formality?

This information will then guide your attitude prior to entering the interview room. To begin with, you will know what to wear. You should know who will be interviewing you – if not the makeup of the whole panel – as then at least you will know that one of the members will be from the recruitment function or the main contact for graduate recruits. Think about the company's image and how you can ensure that your appearance reflects that image. Obviously, consider any guidelines the company offers in this area, but in general, if this is a first and formal interview, regardless of the industry you are working in, you should find a smart and comfortable suit. Don't go overboard either financially or in terms of power dressing – keep it simple. Play around with your interview image days before the meeting takes place. Know what kind of make-up you should apply, make sure the shoes you want to wear are immaculate and even that the socks that match them are clean and ready. Leave nothing to chance, because on the day you are going to be nervous and the last thing you want to be worried about is ironing a shirt.

Arrive in good time for the interview, even if this means that you end up walking round the block two or three times because you're so early. If you're extremely early then find a nearby café, sit down, relax and collect your thoughts. You may want to scan a few interview notes if necessary, but all your preparation in terms of what you want to say should already be rehearsed and playing confidently in your head.

Once inside the interview location, allow the person conducting the interview to control the environment. Someone will lead you into the interview room and make formal introductions. They will invite you to sit down and ensure that everything runs smoothly. Be guided by their words and actions: Don't offer to shake the hand of anyone who isn't obviously intending to shake your hand. Don't try to look the entire interview panel in the eye if some are simply not looking your way. Above all, don't start a conversation. Answer questions, respond to people, but don't instigate a particular subject.

Some believe decisions are made at interviews within the first few seconds. While this may not always be the case, first impressions are very important. You want to come across as professional and confident. If you start talking unbidden about your journey to the interview, or reply to a simple enquiry as to your trip here with a long, in-depth, blow-by-blow account of how traumatic your day has been, you will come across as nervous and jittery. The fact that you are nervous and jittery is taken as read, but you can't afford to show that. If you can't handle the stress of an interview situation, the panel may not believe that you can handle the stress of a normal working day.

Some interviews will be more of an ordeal than others. There are still interviews carried out specifically to see how you operate under pressure and you may find yourself having questions or hypothetical scenarios shot at you and a response expected immediately. It is likely that you will already have knowledge that this will happen, however, so don't go into every interview worried that you're about to be shouted at. On the majority of occasions you'll find that your interviewers want to put you at your ease and want to give you ample opportunity to put your best face forward.

If the interview is run by a panel, direct your answers principally to the person who asks you the question. You can acknowledge other panel members as you talk, but don't pretend you're playing to an audience. By directing your replies to one person you will come across as focused and confident. Moreover, it is likely that that person will ask follow-up questions, so it makes more sense to have a dialogue with that person than with the room in general.

Try not to repeat only what is on your application form. Certainly there will be some cross-over and repetition, but you need to expand on that information – otherwise, why attend the interview in the first place?

At the end of the interview most interviewers will ask you if there's anything you want to ask them. Make sure that you have something to ask and make sure that it isn't a question to which you should already know the answer. Asking precisely what the business of the company is and what your job will be isn't going to impress anyone. Don't press for remuneration details or holiday entitlement at this point – the interviewers may get a warped sense of your priorities.

If nothing else, simply ask what the next stage is in their recruitment process. Find out when you can expect to hear from them and whether there will be any further exercises to complete subsequent to this interview. This will not only give you something definite to take away from the interview, but also gives the impression of an applicant who's got other options available and is figuring out how this current possibility measures up to everything else.

Getting this information clear also means that you will be able to follow up the interview in an efficient and professional manner rather than just calling to see if anyone's made a decision yet.

The CV

If you are asked to send a CV rather than filling in the boxes on an application form, take your time on the presentation of this document. In the age of computer technology, word processors and a truckload of templates, there is no excuse for a badly constructed CV. If you don't have access to a computer that can do this, call up your friendly neighbourhood design and printing company who will lay out the perfect document for you.

Keep the CV relevant and efficient. Only in exceptional cases should the document run to more than two pages. At this stage in your life you should be able to get everything your employer needs to see on one side of A4.

Word processing technology also means that you can tailor your CV to each potential employer. Through a process of cut and paste and the occasional rewording, you can prioritize certain interests, talk up one aspect of your work experience or skills, ensuring that each time you send a CV out, it keys into the aspects your employer is looking for.

Things every CV should have

- Full name.
- Contact address, phone number(s) and e-mail address.
- Date of birth.
- Nationality.

- Education history – usually with the most recent qualification first.
- Work experience – again, usually most recent job first. Feel free to omit 'bar work' in order to draw attention to more relevant jobs or work experience within your chosen industry.
- Other interests – always good to show an enjoyment of sports or other activities which have nothing to do with work, but it's also nice when an extracurricular activity has relevance to the workplace.

Strike a balance between talking yourself up and giving the impression that you're using jargon to mask the less than thrilling reality of your experience. For example, don't describe your past job as 'resource manager' if you simply stacked shelves. Employers know the kind of jobs available to undergraduates and there are still useful skills to be gained from shelf-stacking.

The letter of enquiry

The least structured method of approach, the letter of enquiry will arrive as a bolt out of the blue from you to your hoped-for employer. It must therefore immediately impress the reader, demonstrating that you know their company and what you want to do for them.

Letters of enquiry should be sent to a named person within the organization. Beginning 'Dear Sir/Madam' will not gain you any credentials. You can find the right person to write to by carrying out some basic research: Is the company so small you can write to the managing director? Is there someone in particular in charge of an interesting project?

Tell your reader how you came across their organization and why you decided to write to him or her. This could be something as simple as 'I found your Web site and was impressed by the work you do' or 'I have been following a project you have been doing over the past few months and would love to get involved'. In some instances you might want to risk an approach such as: 'I saw your Web site and believe that I can do a better job of designing your pages', but be careful not to be too critical. After all, you want to work with the reader and deriding his or her performance so far will not give that impression.

The letter of enquiry should be only a page long and should be accompanied by your CV (two pages max.). To get full value from your approach, cross-reference the CV in your letter: 'As you can see, I have had work experience in your industry...'.

Once sent, feel free to follow up your enquiry with a phone call. Give it a few days and don't pester. Ask whether the letter has been received and whether you can expect to hear anything over the next few weeks. In some cases you'll find that the letter has been passed on to the recruitment function – in which case you can be sure that it's gone with the approval of your initial contact at the company.

Letters of enquiry must be tailored to each specific company – throughout the text, not just by updating the address and correspondent details. Be sure to keep copies of those you send out so you know what they know about you when they get in touch.

Feeling confused about what you want to do after university? Joining the Civil Service means you don't have to narrow your options.

There are a number of ways you can join the Civil Service for a range of jobs just too numerous to number! Many don't even involve sitting at desks but are out at airports, living overseas, meeting the public, visiting farms, at sea, working in labs – and only one in five is based in London. Some individual departments offer graduate recruitment schemes and if you have specialist skills, there are even more options – if you're an IT specialist or a linguist, you could work for GCHQ on intelligence gathering, or if you're a trainee solicitor, working for the Government Legal Service. Further internal opportunities are also advertised regularly once you have joined.

The Civil Service is committed to training every member of staff and we even have our own training college. Many civil servants are sponsored by their units to take on further study. As a senior manager, this could mean an MBA or if you're working in marketing, perhaps a course in freelance journalism. Promotion in the Civil Service is always on merit, so you can expect to be rewarded for high-quality work. Departments are responsible for their own salary scales, and many operate bonus schemes and performance related pay, as well as offering flexi time and excellent pensions.

So where do you start? The Recruitment Gateway web site www.careers.civil-service.gov.uk is the best place to begin researching a career with us. You'll find comprehensive information on the work of departments and agencies, links to their websites and contact details. There are a range of recruitment schemes for graduates with specialist as well as generalist skills and also a database of current vacancies that you can apply directly for. It's also a good idea to read both the local and national press regularly for other opportunities.

For talented graduates, there really is a world of choice waiting for you in the Civil Service.

You have a vague idea of what you want to do. We have a firm idea about how far you can grow.

There are hundreds of diverse opportunities available to graduates in the Civil Service. And when you consider the sheer breadth of what we do – from funding European space flight projects to preventing street crime – there's bound to be something to hook you. Whatever direction you do pursue, you can expect the very best in personal and professional development. See our web site for comprehensive details of current vacancies across government – www.careers.civil-service.gov.uk

A world of choice for your career

CIVILSERVICE

11 Graduate recruitment tests

Depending on the size of your future employer (and their recruitment budget), you may be asked to complete a variety of tests prior to being offered a position. Alternatively, you may be offered a position within the company and then be given a whole load of tests to determine precisely where you should fit into the organization and what skills you need to work on during your early days.

These tests could be carried out in a controlled environment – ie as a conventional examination with a certain amount of time to complete – they may be spread out over a number of days and there may even be an 'assessment weekend' in which all new recruits are put through their paces. Increasingly, these kinds of tests can be administered online via a secure Internet Web site but they may also involve pen and paper – multiple choice or longer answers to assess technical knowledge. If your organization has arranged an entire weekend of activities, it is likely that there will be team-based work included, and even outward-bound exercises.

Whatever the method of delivery and format, these tests assess one of two things about you: your ability and your personality.

Ability tests

Ability tests find out what you can do in the widest possible sense. What do you actually know about the company, business and the role you have applied for? How up to date are you with your knowledge and what kind of context do you understand you will be working in? An assessment test might even focus on tasks you will be expected to do in the workplace. There may be something like an 'in-tray' exercise where you are given a typical in-tray full of information and challenges similar to those within the company and asked to work your way through them, deciding what to do with each problem.

There may be role-playing exercises which place you in a scenario where you must negotiate with one or more other participants. This exercise is not a matter of ensuring that you get your own way in a situation, but of demonstrating your ability to work with other people, present your case and reason around an issue. Another exercise might be to present a topic to an assessment panel. This could be something directly relevant to the company, or again a random topic, selected to demonstrate your ability to hold the attention of an audience and explain your subject precisely and clearly.

The closer the tests mirror what you will have to do in a normal working day, the more accurate information your employer will gain to understand your strengths and weaknesses and the more effective support they can give you in the workplace.

In order to be successful, make sure that you have done your research. The interview process will have given you the opportunity to demonstrate your understanding and knowledge of their company, but these tests will let you go further – using that information in a practical way. You should not only research the activities and culture of the company, but also find out as much as you possibly can about the tests you will face. Make sure that you have all the information necessary for the tests. Double-check this information as soon as you receive it and make a note of any preparatory work you should do, such as preparing a five-minute presentation.

If you have the chance, talk to someone who has already been through the process. Careers fairs will usually feature a 'normal' employee from the company, perhaps with two or three years' experience, brought along specifically to tell you what it's like to work in the company. Having grilled them for general information, ask them about the application process and any recruitment tests. The chances are that they will be able to talk freely about the process (while not necessarily giving you tips on how to succeed) and you can use this information to reassure yourself. Even knowing how many tests are carried out, how soon the results are known and if you are ever told directly of the results will enable you to approach the experience with greater confidence.

You should remember that, up to a point, there are no right or wrong answers to these tests. You can research and practise for aspects of an ability test – indeed you must rehearse a presentation over and over again to make sure that you deliver it properly under pressure – but having done that, your ability will be at a certain level, and your employers will work with that. With personality tests, the fact that there are no wrong answers is even more important to bear in mind.

Personality tests

Controversy has always surrounded the concept of personality testing – whether personality can be measured as such and how much importance should be attached to the results. Put simply, these tests take a participant's response to certain situations and statements and create a personality profile based on these responses – an insight into that participant which the employer can use to judge whether that person will fit into their organization or if he or she is the type of person they should be employing anywhere. These tests are usually in the form of multiple choice answers and frequently ask you to record how much or little you agree with certain statements such as 'I like working on my own', 'I enjoy a varied social life' and even 'It is acceptable to break the rules in order to achieve my aims'. Tests can be administered through pen and paper or through secure Internet sites. In both cases participants are given a limited amount of time in which to complete the test.

From a participant's point of view, the key is not to worry about these tests. Make sure that you understand each question entirely and answer them as honestly as possible – which usually means going with your first instinct. Don't try to give the answers you believe your employers want to hear. In the first place, the test manufacturers claim that they have designed these questionnaires to highlight inconsistent answers, thereby identifying respondents who may be trying to impress or cover something up rather than say what they think. In the second place, the test is there to see if you will fit into the organization. If you do not answer the questions honestly and are then successful in joining the company, you may be creating problems for yourself further down the line.

The results of these tests will *never* entirely determine whether your application is successful. Recruiters will take the results into consideration, but they would be foolish to rule out everyone with a certain profile. One of the main reasons for this is that there is no firm link between a personality profile and final performance in a company. One can speculate on the link, but there is no watertight guarantee. It is worth remembering that some tests have found entrepreneurs and high-flying business leaders to have very similar personality profiles to criminals. They share similar attitudes to 'conventional' rules, taking risks and working with people around them.

In all of these tests, you should remember that there is no such thing as a bad or wrong answer. Certainly you may not cover all the points your employers are looking for, you may not measure up to their ideal graduate applicant, but the point is that they need to see who you are. If you demonstrate your skills with confidence, don't make silly mistakes or give the impression that you really couldn't care less, then your employer will know exactly what they are getting. They will be able to determine if you are right for their organization, how you might perform and what kind of support you will need to succeed.

12 Career paths and professional qualifications

Some careers have very clear and definite pathways from first appointment through to senior positions. As a graduate you are likely to start your career in the ranks of lower-level management, rising to middle and senior management and finally to a director or executive-level appointment. However, it is equally possible that your career will not take such a linear course. Many graduates work their way through three or four different jobs in their first years of work – and these jobs are not necessarily even in the same industry. Graduates can find themselves attracted to different industries, inspired by the change of context in which they work as much as by any increase in responsibility.

However, whether you take a linear approach to your career or a more circumlocutory one, you may find that you need to pass yet more exams to prove your professional aptitude. You may need to take exams to gain recognition from professional associations, membership of which will enable you to ascend further up the career ladder and increase your remuneration.

Some career paths are part and parcel of the job you have taken on and your employer will support and guide you through your development – they gain from your increased skill and expertise as much as you do. Accountants, for example, have a whole range of exams to take while working in their first few years. These exams determine precisely what kind of accountancy they are qualified to perform. For managers and business people there are professional qualifications such as the MBA (Masters in Business Administration) which are not compulsory for their work but do prove that the individual has undertaken ongoing education and increased his or her professional skill.

Throughout the workplace there is an increasing awareness of 'life-long learning' – the concept that no one ever stops learning, gaining new skills or knowledge. Indeed, it is argued that no one can afford to stop learning as they need to keep up with the industry in which they work. This awareness is demonstrated clearly within almost every professional representative body through the provision of programmes for continued professional development (CPD).

CPD may consist of a carefully structured roster of courses which professional workers can access and follow, or may simply be a selection of courses from which they can pick and choose according to their particular needs at the time. While employers may offer you some support structures for this kind of development, and signing up for a significant qualification such as an MBA may require you to follow a structured course at your chosen educational institute, you will remain largely responsible for managing your own education, getting motivated and carrying out the work required.

As all areas of business become more competitive, employers will pay premiums for proven talent, which means that if you want to be successful a professional qualification is imperative. You need to find out what qualifications are suitable for you and how you can finance and find time for this education. If your employer does not already provide assistance in this area you should try to convince them that it is in their interests to help you get these skills. If your employer is not interested in supporting your professional development, it is more than likely that you will be able to find an employer who is.

Professional qualifications can provide useful signposts for your career. Even if the promotional ladder within your employer's company or between employers within your industry sector is unclear, identifying and working towards a professional qualification is a good way of focusing your efforts and creating a career structure for yourself. You may not be able to say that in five years' time you will have a certain status with a certain company, but you can state that you will have the right level of skills to fulfil a more senior position when the opportunity arises.

Qualifications are becoming more important to achieving promotion because the opportunities to learn 'on the job' and develop your skills in this way are decreasing. Over the years, companies across every industry sector have slimmed down, becoming streamlined and flexible in order to increase their competitiveness in the market-place. This has meant restructuring the way work is done within an organization and stripping out layers of management which were perceived as contributing little value to the work of the company. What these management layers did offer, however, were regular steps for employees seeking promotion. Once they had excelled in one position it was easy to promote them to the next level since the amount and nature of their responsibility wasn't drastically increased and the company could afford to support any employee who made a mistake at the next step up.

Now, steps between management levels have increased. Gaining promotion can mean taking on an entirely different level and type of responsibility. You may go from being in charge of your own work to being in charge of the work of many other people, without having prior experience of delegating work. To make such a move success-fully you may need to bring into play talents and approaches which you've never previously considered or may not even believe you had.

Professional qualifications are a good way for preparing yourself for such new challenges. MBAs, for example, usually include project work, the subject of which you can determine so that it has direct relevance to your career. This work may be research based and never require you actually to do anything new practically, but it will increase your awareness of how your business works and therefore how you need to adapt in order to meet the challenge of your next promotion.

The career paths of today's employees are as likely to run sideways as they are to go upwards. Again, the reduction of opportunities for straightforward promotion means that employees are as likely to locate their next challenge with a different organization altogether as they are at a different level with their current employer. There may still be an increase in responsibilities and remuneration, but the main attraction will be the variety and newness of the work offered by a different employer. This also illustrates how the creation and following of a career path is now primarily the employees' responsi-bility and subject to their desires and initiative rather than the oppor-tunities provided by their employer.

THE TIMES

2nd edition

odd

jobs

Unusual
ways to earn a living

SIMON KENT

Over the past year or two, accountancy has been placed firmly at the forefront of the business world's agenda. ACCA has taken a significant role in developing the profession in the global marketplace for 100 years and has led the way on issues such as corporate social and environmental responsibility. Our syllabus has advanced in anticipation of industry requirements while still retaining the core technical knowledge invaluable to the modern finance professional.

Each year, over 12,000 graduates join ACCA, because it opens the door to a future that is diverse, challenging and constantly surprising. It is also a future that offers the very real opportunity to become an influential figure in business. We work with key employers through our Employer Accreditation Scheme, recognising their commitment to supporting ACCA students through their qualification. Abbey National plc, Accenture, Arcadia Group plc, Barclays plc, BBC, British Airways, Capital One, Centrica plc, Debenhams, HBOS, Marks & Spencer, Standard Chartered Bank and TXU Europe are amongst the many high-profile recruiters who hold ACCA Gold or Platinum Approved Accredited Employer status.

Flexibility and choice

ACCA's study and training are designed to be as flexible as possible – offering you real choices. With the widest range of study options and an unrivalled dedication to utilising new technologies, your progress through the qualification can be as flexible as you need it to be. Most significantly, you have the freedom to gain your work experience in public practice or in the public or corporate sectors, and are able to change both employer and sector should you desire a broader base of experience. This is supported by a syllabus that is unique in offering specialist papers, ensuring you gain a solid foundation of financial knowledge as well as a firm grounding in the broader-based business skills that will prepare you for senior financial and management positions. It represents the ultimate in integrity, flexibility and true vocational opportunity.

Practical experience

The theme of flexibility continues into the practical experience requirements. The application of your theoretical knowledge in the workplace is crucial to the development of the management, personal and technical skills that are central to career success as an ACCA accountant. The three years relevant supervised experience can take place before, during or after the ACCA study and examinations.

Employers value the all-round financial expertise provided by ACCA's professional qualification. Pan Philippou, Managing Director for Diesel UK describes ACCA as "nstantly recognisable around the world, a first class indication of professional competence in the world of finance and accounting". For him, his ACCA qualification contributed directly to his career development: "The diversity of the companies that I worked for underlines the portability of the qualification that finally led me to Diesel and the world of fashion".

Qualified for life

There is also the opportunity to study for further ACCA qualifications, including specialist diplomas and the uniquely tailored MBA. ACCA is the first professional body to design an MBA specifically for finance professionals, ensuring our members have the opportunity to develop those skills most essential to their business careers.

The efficient use of financial information is crucial to business success. Accountants hold the key for many businesses, with company directors relying on their finance professionals to help them formulate business strategies and steer them through new economic, legislative and commercial risks. ACCA is committed to providing the expertise they require to remain competitive.

For more information on the opportunities ACCA can offer, visit **www.accaglobal.com**, contact us on **0141 582 2000** or email **students@accaglobal.com**

Because I want my qualifications to take me places.
Not just to work and back.

If you are a graduate keen to develop your career in accountancy, the ACCA qualification will open doors across the world. And after you've qualified, our ongoing development programme will help to keep your skills up to speed as you work your way up in your chosen field.

To find out more about what ACCA could do for your career visit www.accaglobal.com or contact us on tel: +44 (0)141 582 2000 fax: +44 (0)141 582 2222 e-mail: students@accaglobal.com

Qualified for life

13 Employment opportunities in selected areas

Industry

Graduates from any discipline can find a challenging and fulfilling first job within industry. There are opportunities which might take advantage of your particular specialism – science and engineering degrees can help in the development and manufacture of a range of products – or alternatively, your degree will simply be regarded as a mark of professional ability and intelligence by employers seeking out good management talent.

The decline of UK industry has been a theme visited by the media time and again over the past few years, and while it is true that there has been a decline in the number of products actually made within the UK, graduates should not believe that the only future lies in the service industries. The fact is that with the rise of small and medium-sized manufacturing companies, together with mergers, acquisitions and the globalization of industry, the sector still offers some of the best graduate opportunities in terms of high levels of responsibility early on in your career as well as a future full of challenge.

Main industry trends

The key to successful modern industry is 'just in time'. This means that in all stages of the manufacturing process, deliveries occur as close as possible to the time when demand for that delivery occurs. For example, if you are producing electronic consumer goods and need to supply them to high-street department stores, you should make sure that your delivery arrives at the store just as the store sells the last of its previous stock. Similarly, within your own factory where the goods are produced, you should ensure that raw materials arrive just at the point when you require those items for the manufacturing process. In both cases, this ensures that the business maximizes returns from its resources – there is no time wasted waiting for supplies to arrive and little warehouse space wasted in stockpiling raw materials or finished items.

There's no getting away from the fact that industry is a global concern. In every sector, there are examples where manufacturing can be carried out at a lower cost offshore than at a location within the UK. For this reason, creating and distributing a product has become a great challenge in terms of logistics. A company may assemble its products in a different location from where those components were created. Ensuring that quality standards are met along the way requires the design and implementation of global strategies while managing production on a worldwide scale – communicating between different parts of the workforce or between outsourcing organizations is also a challenge.

In many parts of UK industry there is now a recognition that companies cannot compete on price alone – there is always going to be an international company or importer that can do the same job for less money. As a result, competitive advantage lies in creating products of greater value and higher quality. Companies therefore need to be sure of their unique selling point in this respect and ensure that their customers are well aware of the benefits available through their organization.

There are increasing opportunities for 'niche marketing' products to very specific customer groups. At the same time, some consumers are aware of the global nature of manufacturing and have negative responses to arrangements that appear to exploit cheap labour in some parts of the world or processes that impact negatively on the environment. Ethical industry makes extra challenges on business managers to deliver a competitively priced product while controlling the potential damage inflicted by their activities.

Large industrial employers used to provide a huge number of secure jobs for many people – sometimes whole communities relied on one particular industry, and indeed company, for sustenance.

Today, it is recognized that there are no jobs for life. In addition, the diversification of the workforce means that industry needs to offer increased opportunities for flexible working if it is to access the most effective and talented members of the working population. This means that organizing the way work is done – from rostering shifts to creating reward packages – has become an art in itself. People management in industry is growing in profile as more employers realize that the workforce is their greatest asset. Functions such as recruitment and retention, for example, can be very expensive for organizations if they cannot attract or keep the personnel they need to operate.

Ways into the workplace

Large manufacturers have both the scale and resources to offer graduates places on induction courses which introduce graduates to their business and set them on the road to achieving a professional position in a short number of years.

These courses give a wide-ranging view of company operations and can be linked to the achievement of relevant professional qualifications. There is usually an opportunity for graduate recruits to demonstrate their enthusiasm and skills through personal projects aimed at identifying potential efficiencies within current processes. In this way, companies gain returns on their graduate investment at the earliest opportunity. As time goes by, you will increasingly specialize in your industry, concentrating on managing an area such as supply chain management, people management or process management.

Smaller companies employ graduates with the expectation that they can find their feet quickly and start contributing to the business almost immediately. There may be less teaching and more learning-by-doing with such companies and you may find yourself immediately faced with a live business problem which requires you to work with other managers in order to move the company forward. Whatever the size of your employer, it is imperative that you identify with the company culture if you are to work effectively and have a positive experience in your first job.

Professional bodies offering jobs, information and further education

The Chartered Management Institute
Management House, Cottingham Road, Corby, Northamptonshire
NN17 1TT; Tel: 01536 204222; www.inst-mgt.org.uk.
Continuous professional development, career information and useful networking organization.

Chartered Institute of Personnel and Development
CIPD House, Camp Road, Wimbledon, London SW19 4UX;
Tel: 020 8971 9000; www.cipd.co.uk.

The Institute of Operations Management
University of Warwick Science Park, Sir William Lyons Road,
Coventry CV4 7EZ; Tel: 024 7669 2266; www.iomnet.org.uk.
Awards certificates, diplomas and offers careers information.

Chartered Institute of Purchasing and Supply
Easton House, Easton on the Hill, Stamford, Lincolnshire PE9 3NZ;
Tel: 01780 756777; www.cips.org.
Professional certification, continuous professional development and careers resource.

The Institute of Logistics and Transport
11/12 Buckingham Gate, London SW1E 6LB; Tel: 01536 740100;
www.iolt.org.uk.
Certificate, diploma qualifications and networking opportunities for industry professionals.

Consultancy

Consultants have come to play an important and increasing role in many aspects of the UK workplace. While the subject of ridicule in some quarters – there's a general feeling that consultants are frequently paid for coming into an organization and stating the obvious, or that they are brought in to carry out radical procedures before leaving the organization in disarray – they do provide essential services to many businesses.

The principal strength of being a consultant is the independent view you can bring to each situation you are faced with. This independence means that you can understand and feed back to an organization precisely what is going on in its business and see where processes are failing. You can then suggest changes to enhance the business. Sometimes consultants have a legal inspection and audit role – such as Health and Safety consultants – and in such situations their perceptions and recommendations on a specific situation can have far-reaching effects for an organization.

Main industry trends

Consultants work in both the private and public sectors. To some extent, the slimming down and streamlining of organizations has meant that certain skills are no longer retained by organizations and instead they need to bring in external experts to provide that input. Ironically, consultants are often blamed for suggesting redundancies and streamlining organizations, which then further necessitates their use.

Within the public sector, consultants have been involved in the management of contracts between private and public organizations concerning services to be delivered, building and maintenance programmes. Their role has been to identify precisely what work needs to be done and to ensure that all parties understand what is required of their working relationship. They ensure that performance standards are met. Consultants are often used to make communications between public and private sector organizations easier.

Given the scepticism that many consultants face, it is imperative that workers in this area have a professional approach at all times. Consultancy companies and individual consultants need to be sure to gain credibility with their clients and this can only be done through establishing a clear and consistent track record as well as through professional qualifications and membership of appropriate representative bodies. These latter organizations usually demand that members adhere to a code of professional conduct and can be the gateway to professional training and qualifications.

People skills are key to working as a consultant. No matter what you are consulting on and no matter how much knowledge and information you have at your disposal, unless you can convince your client – and more importantly, their employees – that your suggestion is the way ahead, you will generate resentment and resistance which can be more detrimental to an organization than if you had never intervened. Every project undertaken must have a clear start point and objective, with all parties understanding what a successful intervention looks like and what will happen after the consultants finish their work. The worst thing that can happen is that an organization becomes dependent upon its consultants in order to make everyday decisions.

One other aspect of consultancy is one-on-one support. Employees in senior positions such as chief executives or managing directors may need support in the form of mentoring or coaching in order to keep a fresh perspective on their work. Again, these kinds of personal development/support roles tend to be carried out by experienced and senior consultants. In these types of role it is less important that you know the nitty gritty of your coachee's business, just that you can understand and relate to the type of problems he or she is facing.

Ways into the workplace

Most consultants are expected to reach their position via a number of management positions which have given them experience and key skills within their sector. However, there are also large business consultancy firms who take on graduates and put them through a full induction course, enabling them to start operating within client companies at the earliest opportunity. While detractors argue that such consultants are simply given the consultant companies' generic approach and then encouraged to apply this approach across the board, it can equally be argued that after such training, new consultants can provide a valuable and consistent approach to each problem they encounter. While their approach may be the same, the solutions they provide will be different for each client.

There are an increasing number of small consulting companies, many of which offer specific services for specific clients. These organizations have fewer vacancies but can offer greater challenges to graduates, keying into your own interests in a more satisfying way than working for a larger firm. Smaller-scale operations also enable you to get more deeply involved with clients than would be the case if you were working as part of a larger team.

Alternatively, graduates may find that they already have the skills and knowledge required to contribute as a consultant. Your experience as an undergraduate, perhaps through extracurricular activities such as editing the student magazine or handling student union affairs, may have given you sufficient knowledge to be able to approach a range of organizations with your skills. You may already have experience in the field of fundraising through charity work or organizing charity events and therefore be able to work as a consultant in this field.

Consultancy offers a way of specializing in a certain skill or subject area without limiting yourself to one workplace. True, you may end up working for a consulting company, but your work there will be project related, with diverse clients rather than one single ongoing programme of work.

Professional bodies offering jobs, information and further education

Management Consultancies Association
49 Whitehall, London SW1A 2BX; Tel: 020 7321 3990;
www.mca.org.uk.
Requires three years' work before membership, but also offers news and careers information.

Public Relations Consultants Association
Willow House, Willow Place, Victoria, London SW1P 1JH;
Tel: 020 7233 6026; www.martex.co.uk/prca/index.htm.
Careers, jobseeker service and training information.

Chemical and Industrial Consultants Association
The CICA Honorary Secretary, 6 Church Bank, Richmond Road,
Bowden, Cheshire WA14 3NW; Tel: 0161 928 6681;
www.chemical-consultants.co.uk.
Membership, training, news and jobs.

Association of Fundraising Consultants
The Grove, Harpenden, Hertfordshire AL5 1AH; Tel: 01582 762446;
www.afc.org.uk.
Representing body for fundraising consultants plus tips on best practice.

Independent Safety Consultants Association
PO Box 5940, Hinckley, Leicestershire LE10 1WA;
Tel: 01455 897043; www.isca.org.uk.
Professional training and certification for consultants and inspectors,
plus database of consultants in safety across business sectors.

Financial services and accountancy

Accountancy, financial management, investment, commercial and
even retail banking may initially strike you as purely numerically
based sectors. However, every financial transaction has a human
dimension – be it someone's pay packet, investment in a new
product or business, or the increase in value of someone's savings.
Making the right links between financial and business goals is key to
success within the financial services sector. Often regarded as a dry
area of work, finance professionals can find themselves at the cutting
edge of business, making top-level decisions within organizations, or
at least giving the go-ahead for important initiatives to take place.

Naturally, the legal and bureaucratic side of the job is something
that cannot be avoided, and it is refreshing to find that the careers
Web site of one major accountancy firm freely admits that every day
is not going to be different for graduate recruits at their company. To
be successful in this industry you need to be a meticulous and exact
worker, as keen on making sure that the details add up as you are
keen to take on large and innovative projects.

Main industry trends

Large accountancy firms have proven extremely good graduate
employers – not simply for the size and type of remuneration, but
also for the working culture they now offer. Since competition for

highly qualified graduates is so intense, accountancy firms have addressed their company culture to attract the best. This includes relaxed dress codes and flexible working, even the provision of 'gap years' to enable employees to go travelling for a number of months and return to their original position.

Recent headline news stories have demonstrated how important it is to have accurate accounts. Graduates can find themselves working within multinational organizations that employ tens of thousands of people worldwide. Making sure that the financial support for these companies is in place is a crucial task.

In recent years, the poor performance of the stock market has made the work of traders and investment managers far harder. Recruitment has fallen and in some areas, financial rewards have been reduced. Success as an investment analyst or fund manager comes down to understanding how each business sector operates and making an accurate assessment of the potential future performance of individual companies. If your clients are expecting a high return on their investment, it is clear that your performance will only be judged by the increased financial value you achieve.

The growth of small to medium-sized enterprises (SMEs) and the self-employed across the economy has supported the work of personal and small-scale accountancy firms in areas such as tax advice and company audits. It is possible that you can work towards a high-level position such as financial director of a small company, or you may be able to establish yourself as a specialist consultant working for a variety of small businesses. In general, it is best to establish yourself within a particular business sector so you can offer clients a dedicated financial service tailored to the requirements of their particular sector.

Ways into the workplace

High street banks – that is, the area of banking with which you will be most familiar – are also known as the retail banking sector and unsurprisingly have many jobs in common with the retail sector. Here the emphasis is on developing and providing financial products to customers – attractive bank accounts, savings facilities, mortgages, loans and so on. Many high street banks run graduate training

Red hot business leaders?

The ACA qualification

If you're planning to become one of tomorrow's red hot business leaders, start by following the path taken by around 3,000 of the sharpest young minds every year. The Institute of Chartered Accountants in England & Wales' ACA qualification. As the number one financially based business qualification, it leads to a whole host of exciting, demanding and rewarding careers. To begin exploring the world of colour opened up by the ACA, go to **www.icaew.co.uk/careers**

The full spectrum without the grey

THE INSTITUTE OF
CHARTERED
ACCOUNTANTS

IN ENGLAND & WALES

The full spectrum without the grey

Chartered Accountancy has undergone a quiet revolution. It's always been an important profession, since it underpins the smooth running of just about every organisation out there. But recently, technological advances have enabled computers to crunch the numbers, leaving Chartered Accountants free to concentrate their efforts on deciding where organisations are heading and how best to get there.

Viewed as a 'mark of quality' by employers, the ACA (Associate Chartered Accountant) qualification allows graduates to create some distance from their peers. Best of all, it's a profession that's as far-reaching as it is direct. Qualified Chartered Accountants work as professional business advisers in every size of organisation, in all spheres of business and the public sector.

Where could it take you?

Chartered Accountants work at the cutting edge of business and industry and have a far-reaching impact on the strategies of organisations throughout the world. They are the people who make the high-level strategic decisions that improve profitability and increase market share. Some 80% of FTSE 100 companies have at least one Chartered Accountant on the board, as Chief Executive Officer or as Finance Director.

Around half of all ACAs work in public practice as partners or employees in accountancy firms, or as sole practitioners, offering fee-paying client services ranging from audit and tax to management and forensic accounting.

Many others go into industry and commerce, where the opportunities are just as varied. Every business needs a financial guru, and as an ACA that kind of prestige puts you in demand just about anywhere. You can get an idea of the breadth of career paths open to you with this list of some current ACAs' roles:

Deputy Chief Executive of an FA Barclaycard Premiership football club • Chief Executive of an international conglomerate • Chief Executive of an energy and utilities group • Controller of a management consultancy firm • Deputy Chairman of a motor manufacturing group • Director of a high tech company • European Finance Director of a global advertising agency.

An increasing number of ACAs are moving into the public sector, where they're taking on roles such as Directors of Finance at a Strategic Health Authority and an NHS Trust or Area Accountant at the Inland Revenue

If we've opened your eyes to the possibilities of becoming a red hot business leader, you should get in touch with the ICAEW, you'll find our contact details on the advert opposite.

THE INSTITUTE OF
CHARTERED
ACCOUNTANTS

IN ENGLAND & WALES

schemes similar to those operated by retail and supermarket chains – with experience on the shop floor or with back-office functions acting as a precursor to specializing in a more strategic or managerial role within the company.

Large accountancy firms offer extremely attractive positions to well-qualified graduates and the best applicants can shop around for a remuneration package that suits them. Induction programmes may include experience across the organization's operations and attachments to specific projects. However you begin your career, you will be expected to continue to study for professional qualifications, which may direct you towards specialisms within the industry. The large firms also enjoy an international presence so you may need to be ready to travel in order to take advantage of all the opportunities open to you.

Within large commercial banks, finance experts are employed to take care of the concerns of large companies. This can mean ensuring that their cash flow is sufficient to maintain operations and it can also mean making sure that any money the business has spare is invested wisely and is working for the company rather than lying dormant.

Investors also need highly knowledgeably personnel to understand and invest in the stock exchange, and within the personal banking sector there are all sorts of market analysts, traders and portfolio managers who monitor the changes in the stock market, and advise and act upon these changes in order to increase the value of their customers' investment.

Financial experts also operate within the public sector, perhaps most obviously within tax assessment and collecting operations. The Inland Revenue requires finance experts to analyse and assess tax claims as well as to detect and prosecute possible cases of fraud. At the same time, accountants and auditors are used across the public sector in a variety of ways in order to ensure that public bodies operate correctly and spend public finances wisely.

In an ever more competitive world where profit margins are constantly being pushed back, financial experts have a great deal of status within all organizations. They are key to ensuring that an organization of any size can function in the present day and will have the finance for a successful future.

Professional bodies offering jobs, information and further education

Inland Revenue Fast Stream Recruitment
Personnel Division, Mowbray House, PO Box 55, Castle Meadow
Road, Nottingham NG2 1BE; Tel: 0115 974 0603.
Inland Revenue applications from graduates.

Capita RAS
3rd Floor, Dean Bradley House, 52 Horseferry Road, London SW1P
2AF; www.rasnet.co.uk.
Primary recruiter for public sector positions.

Association of Chartered Certified Accountants (ACCA)
29 Lincoln's Inn Fields, London WC2A 3EE; Tel: 020 7396 7000;
www.acca.org.uk.
Jobs, career development and qualifications.

Institute of Chartered Accountants in England and Wales (ICAEW)
Chartered Accountants Hall, PO Box 433, London EC2P 2BJ;
www.iceaw.co.uk.
Careers, training and vacancies.

The law

In an increasingly litigious society, knowledge of diverse aspects
of the law is of benefit in a number of different employment
sectors. Obviously, graduates who have already taken law as
their first degree will have priority for the best jobs, and may
already have determined their own career path and specialisms.
However, graduates with other qualifications can find themselves
careers within the legal framework following further study on a
course such as a law diploma or Common Professional Examination
(CPE).

   While the law can be viewed as a stringent and exacting area of
practice, there is variety to the work as employees come into contact
with a diverse range of people – whether cases concern private

individuals or commercial organizations. In every case the challenge exists to ensure that clients receive a fair hearing and effective representation so that the problems they encounter can be moved to a satisfactory resolution.

Main industry trends

Successive governments bring in new legislation which impacts on the legal profession. Whenever such legislation occurs, the legal system must be ready to take on these new elements and incorporate them into practice. Since the legal system is independent of the government this is not always a straightforward process and there have been instances when government and legal system have not seen eye to eye. For example, the government may seek to increase penalties for certain crimes in order to reduce the incidence of those crimes. While the courts may uphold this move, it may be that doing so increases the workload of the legal system, resulting in more delays for convictions and an overburdened police and prison service. With crime and disorder such a strong political weapon, the law profession can find itself subject to a great deal of public analysis and debate.

In an attempt to reduce the amount and cost of litigation in business and other disputes, the practice of alternative disputes resolution (ADR) has gained popularity in recent years. ADR includes techniques such as mediation, conciliation and early neutral evaluation. These techniques are intended to avoid official legal proceedings through the courts. A technique such as mediation also keeps a dispute confidential and so the trauma of having details of a case made public and covered by the press is avoided. These techniques can be used for both business and personal disputes and law professionals are training to add recognized skills in these areas to their own legal knowledge in order to offer clients a range of services when disputes are brought to them.

The legal system, like many areas of the public service, is currently undergoing a huge reorganization and modernization process. There are initiatives under way to use communications technology in the court environment – permitting witnesses and suspects to give evidence via closed circuit television, for example, or using digital display screens to present evidence to juries. At the same time, there are moves afoot to bring the Crown Prosecution Service closer to the police service so that prosecution cases can be integrated with the gathering of evidence and questioning of suspects.

Large companies and organizations will employ law specialists on a permanent basis in order to monitor and oversee the legality of their operations and procedures on a day-to-day basis. This could mean taking on an employment law specialist to ensure that all members of a large diverse workforce are properly treated, and that employment policies are in place to protect the company in all eventualities. Alternatively, a media company such as a music publisher or a newspaper may employ specialist lawyers to take care of publishing rights, copyright matters and curb any potential litigious publication. Employment of this kind is becoming more important as technology such as the Internet has increased the ease with which copyright can be breached.

Ways into the workplace

If you do not already have a law-related qualification, that must be top of your hit list upon graduation. You can find a suitable CPE (Common Professional Examination) course or law diploma through the contacts listed below. You should also find yourself work experience within a lawyer's or solicitor's practice in order to see the everyday work of these people. Opportunities exist both within private practices and within the public sector. If you are unable to find this kind of opportunity, you may still find a paralegal role – related but non-legal work – which will give you an insight and a foot in the door to the profession.

You should determine what kind of role you want within the legal profession as soon as possible. You need to tailor your experience and qualifications to a selected area of practice – be it human rights legislation or employment law. If you intend to become a business lawyer or someone who works within a specific industry, you need to gain experience and knowledge of that industry. This may come through your first degree (eg an engineering graduate may ultimately work on the legal side of town and country planning), but may also require that you take a different job within that industry to get background knowledge before making a move towards playing a legal role.

You must be ready to work alongside a wide range of people, whatever position you intend to take. On the one hand you will need to be able to apply strict legal principles to a given situation and explain these to other professional colleagues. As a barrister you will need to be able to present your arguments to a judge or jury. At the same time you need to be able to strike up a rapport with your clients, whoever they may be. Clients will come to you at a time of stress and high emotions and the greatest challenge can lie in managing those emotions effectively in order to get the appropriate outcome.

Professional bodies offering jobs, information and further education

General Council of the Bar
3 Bedford Row, London WC1R 4DB; Tel: 020 7242 0082;
www.barcouncil.org.uk.
News and insight into the work of barristers, including qualifications and careers advice.

Government Legal Service
For the GLS Qualified Recruitment Scheme contact:
Capita RAS, Innovation Court, New Street, Basingstoke, Hampshire RG21 7JB; Tel: 01325 745070.
For GLS trainees and placements contact:
GLS Secretariat, Queen Anne's Chambers, 28 Broadway, London SW1H 9JS; Tel: 020 7210 3304; www.gls.gov.uk.

Institute of Legal Executives
Kempston Manor, Kempston, Bedfordshire MK42 7AB;
Tel: 01234 841000; www.ilex.org.uk.
Training and professional body for legal representatives.

The Law Society
The Law Society Hall, 113 Chancery Lane, London WC2A 1PL;
Tel: 020 7242 1222; www.lawsoc.org.uk.

Information and news from the sector plus continuous professional development and training.

Also:
www.infolaw.co.uk – portal for law resources, including lists of solicitors' practices etc.
www.lcan.csu.ac.uk – Law Careers Advice Network.

The media

One of the most popular areas of work, the media is also one of the least secure employers. Competition throughout the sector is fierce and workers tend to be judged on the success of their most recent project. The media is extremely susceptible to changes in public taste, so a high-performing publication, TV programme, Web site or film company could still face problems if popular culture and taste move on without them.

Perhaps more than in any other industry, career success is a matter of who you know as much as what you know. While there is undoubtedly a sense of 'jobs for the boys/girls' it is also a factor of the pressure under which the industry operates. Given the choice, professionals would far rather work with someone they know or who has been recommended and whose track record is proven elsewhere. Relying on a complete unknown is the last resort.

Many workers in the media are freelance – both on the perfor-mance side of the industry and in the production disciplines. However, the BBC can still offer full-time and fairly long-term employment, while many new independent production companies can also offer long-term employment to successful production and management staff.

Main industry trends

There has been a huge expansion in the number of media channels accessible to the general public. Cable and satellite television, digital radio and the Internet are all providing platforms through which entertainment and information are delivered to the public. Content is also evolving. Creating a popular service now requires close attention to style and tone – to ensure that the programme is accessible, exciting and informative.

Many TV companies are after the 'killer format' – a programme that captures the imagination of the public and pulls in viewers on a regular basis. In recent years the idea of the 'actuality competition' show has dominated television. In these shows – from *Big Brother* through to *Popstars – The Rivals* – the idea is to take members of the public, put them through a series of tests and situations and film their reactions. Crucial to the success of these shows has been the provision of audience interaction, enabling them to vote for whom they think should or shouldn't win. As a mark of how public tastes have changed, a few years ago the 'killer format' for TV appeared to be the 'docusoap' – a documentary programme which centred on the everyday lives of certain people (airport workers, driving instructors, traffic wardens etc) and told their stories in a soap opera format.

With the rise of the Internet, media companies are looking to increase the number of crossover points between each delivery platform. Every broadcaster has their own presence on the Internet and very often individual programmes will have official Web pages dedicated to them, providing viewers with more information on the show and the chance to interact with actors, presenters and writers. This kind of crossover will increase, as will interactive television in general. As viewers become more accepting of the possibilities of interactive TV they will be given increased choice of how to view the programmes broadcast – selecting camera angles, on-screen information and even which character they want to follow in a particular story.

At one time, the print media – newspapers and magazines – were considered to be under threat from the Internet. It was thought that everyone would access the news they required via their home computer or on portable devices. While electronic media is certainly popular, there is still a market for paper-based resources. Indeed, the proliferation of magazines that provide information on gaming technology and home computers suggests that even the most 'wired' individuals still prefer to get some information via the printed page. New technology evangelists may forecast significant changes in the way we receive information in the future, but there will always be something temporary about electronically based formats.

Technology is also creating new opportunities in the film industry. Digital format cameras and editing equipment is putting high-quality recording and editing equipment into the hands of practically anyone. Already there have been blockbuster films made on extremely low budgets where the surrounding hype has more than made up for the lack of promotional finance.

The music industry has also been greatly affected by new technology. While relatively cheap digital recording technology means that anyone can now produce a potentially chart-topping song from the comfort of their own home computer, the Internet and MP3 files enable budding musicians to share their music around the world, creating a 'cult' following without the need for record company involvement. The rise of 'niteclubbing' and the associated culture around this is also enormously lucrative and offers graduates who are switched on to the scene great opportunities to make money while having great fun.

Ways into the workplace

Work experience is crucial to gaining a footing in the media – no matter what your chosen field or employer. In the TV industry it is expected that newcomers start by working for very little money or even for free, as a runner (general dogsbody). Your reward for this hard work and tea-making is that you get to see how the industry operates from the inside. You will see the process behind putting together a TV programme, whether it be from an editorial point of view – from researching a subject through to directing a shoot – or from a post-production role, editing the programme and preparing it for broadcast.

While you will be able to build a stable and clear reputation for yourself by working up through the industry, it is also possible to break into the industry at a high level if you have the energy, confidence and audacity to do it. The public want to be sold the next best thing and love the idea that they know about something hot and new before everyone else does. With the right publicity and management – self-management as much as external guidance – you can set yourself up as the next big thing, whether in the world of popular music, screen writing or journalism.

If the TV and visual media rely on work experience for successful applicants, the print media also require clear skills and vocational training for those who want to get to the top of the editorial tree. True, you can always set up your own publication and learn the skills as you go along, but knowing how to take shorthand notes or how to navigate your way around the software packages now used in many publishing companies will set you ahead of the pack in the real world.

Professional bodies offering jobs, information and further education

The Society for Editors and Proofreaders
Riverbank House, 1 Putney Bridge Approach, Fulham, London SW6 3JD; Tel: 020 7736 3278; www.sfep.org.uk.
Resources including training and freelance work techniques.

Broadcasting Entertainment Cinematograph and Theatre Union (BECTU)
373–377 Clapham Road, London SW9 9BT; Tel: 020 7346 0900; www.bectu.org.uk.
Union for workers in the broadcast and entertainment industry offering workplace support and training. Web site includes extensive links page to other useful sites.

FT2 – Film and Television Freelance Funding
4th Floor, Warwick House, 9 Warwick Street, London W1R 5RA; www.ft2.org.uk.
Courses and placements in all parts of the visual media.

BBC Recruitment
PO Box 7000, London W12 8ZL; Tel: 020 8225 9883; www.bbc.co.uk/jobs/.
Be aware that recruitment addresses and contacts can vary between departments and roles.

SkillSet
124 Horseferry Road, London SW1P 2TX; Tel: 020 7306 8585;
www.skillset.org.
Training body for professionals in film, TV and interactive media.

British Film Institute
21 Stephen Street, London W1T 1LN; Tel: 020 7255 1444;
www.bfi.org.uk/education/study/skillset.
Database of training opportunities.

National Union of Journalists
308 Gray's Inn Road, London WC1X 8DP; www.nuj.org.uk.
Training links and trade body for print media workers.

Healthcare

Many graduates set on a career in the health service will have already determined their path. They will have undergone five years of medical training at an undergraduate level, or seven years if they hope to work in a hospital rather than at General Practice level. However, there are many opportunities in the healthcare sector for graduates whose first degree is not health related. These positions may include the management of people and processes, IT-related roles and disciplines such as information collection and analysis.

While the NHS remains one of the UK's largest employers, the health sector now encompasses a wide range of private sector employers as well, offering services from business consultation through to private nursing and the design and provision of health monitoring equipment. Whatever your position or employer, a successful career in the health service requires a level of dedication and self-sacrifice that is not always seen in other professions. Since the overall aim of your work is to make people better and to improve the general health of the population, it is difficult to leave workplace issues in the workplace and not be concerned about these issues during your time off.

Main industry trends

The NHS is currently undergoing a major modernization programme which the government hopes will create a health service that delivers its services efficiently and is accessible to as many UK residents as possible. There is an extensive IT investment programme underway which involves a huge amount of money being spent on systems and technology to enhance the delivery of healthcare. Alongside this is a restructuring programme which some have described as the biggest management challenge to exist in the world today. Responsibility for fund holding is shifting between organizations, new mechanisms are being created to measure performance and even the procedures carried out for particular patients and conditions are being assessed and redesigned. Everyone in the health service – from IT managers to nursing staff – will be affected by these changes over the next few years.

The public have increased access to healthcare information. While this should inevitably lead to a healthier population in general, perhaps helping people to lead healthier lives, at the moment it is resulting in more informed and demanding patients. Members of the public can now turn up at their doctor's surgery or hospital consultant's room armed with information on their condition and how best to deal with that condition, all downloaded from the Internet. Staff on the front line in all health organizations are faced with limited resources and so stand little chance of providing the treatment prescribed by this information. Managing patient expectations is therefore as much a part of the job as dealing with the condition of the patient itself.

The current UK population is ageing, which will put greater stress on elderly patient care and related social services in the future. There is a concerted move towards the use of monitoring technology in order to provide adequate care of the elderly – but this is only one area of care which will need to expand to meet future demand.

The healthcare sector produces extremely good headlines for the media and rarely a week goes by without the sector making the news in some shape or other. In spite of the excellent work carried out by the sector, the majority of these stories are negative – highlighting alleged failures of processes, poor quality procedures or apparent inadequacies in healthcare. The fact is that the sector will never have enough resources to satisfy everyone – hard choices have to be made in terms of where treatment should be targeted and how conditions should be managed. Healthcare workers need to be prepared to make tough decisions in this area and constantly face ethical and moral dilemmas.

There is a push towards enhancing preventative care within communities rather than simply dealing with conditions as they arise. This means that organizations such as NHS Trusts must closely analyse health issues in their geographical areas and introduce initiatives to target such trends. One Trust may introduce an awareness programme to combat coronary heart disease, for example, promoting health among their population and reducing the instances of heart attacks with which their hospitals have to deal. Such strategic approaches sometimes require skills from outside the medical profession to ensure that health campaigns and information reach the population as a whole.

Complementary medicine can also offer graduate opportunities. While these disciplines can suffer from lack of credibility, there is a growing demand for acupuncture, homeopathy and osteopathy. Practitioners in this area generally need to undergo specialist training which can take time and be very expensive. Complementary medicine also usually means being self-employed and so you would need to attract and manage your own patients if you are to be successful. These practices are gaining favour among some doctors and general practitioners and in the future some may enjoy official recognition from the British Medical Association.

Ways into the workplace

Graduates may find initial positions within the health service which do not demand specialist qualifications or additional tuition. Some nursing homes will take graduates who demonstrate motivation and aptitude for the job regardless of the subject of their degree. Such work should not be undertaken lightly. Nursing in any context – hospital patients, the elderly or mentally ill – requires an incredible

94   Going to work

amount of patience and understanding. You may also find yourself working unsociable hours and in difficult circumstances. You will need to be mentally and emotionally strong yourself in order to work in this way for any period of time.

Whether you have come into the sector through medical education or via a different discipline, continuous professional development is essential to your career. Without official recognition of your medical skills you will find it difficult to proceed up the career ladder or even between employers. There are a wide range of vocational qualifications available, some of which will key into your current work, and some that will give you new skills and open doors to new areas of work.

You will find that medical knowledge is necessary whichever part of the health sector you are dealing with. Even if you operate as an information manager or a technology consultant providing IT support to a healthcare organization, you will suffer from lack of credibility if you do not appreciate the circumstances in which your clients are operating. While dealing with sick people at the work face requires limitless patience, dealing with the healthcare sector itself is not for the easily deterred.

Professional bodies offering jobs, information and further education

British Acupuncture Council
63 Jeddo Road, London W12 9HQ; Tel: 020 8735 0400;
www.acupucture.org.uk.
Courses for and official register of acupuncturists.

Society of Homeopaths
2 Artizan Road, Northampton NN1 4HU; Tel: 01604 621400;
www.homeopathy-soh.org.

Nursing and Midwifery Admission Service
NMAS, Rosehill, New Barn Lane, Cheltenham, Gloucestershire
GL52 3LZ; Tel: 0870 1122206; www.nmas.ac.uk.
Resource for qualifications for graduates (and undergraduates) in nursing.

The British Diatetic Association
5th Floor Charles House, 148/9 Great Charles Street, Queensway,
Birmingham B3 3HT; Tel: 0121 2008080; www.bda.uk.com.
Vacancies and career advice plus qualification for dieticians.

British Medical Association
BMA House, Tavistock Square, London WC1H 9JP;
Tel: 020 73874499; www.bma.org.uk.
Industry news, careers advice and professional representative body
for medical professionals.

Teaching

Whatever the circumstances in which you are working, teaching is
one of the most rewarding careers you can follow. It's not simply the
kick you get out of imparting wisdom to your students and seeing
their understanding and skills develop and grow, but teaching allows
you to get a closer understanding of your own subject. By finding
new ways of explaining topics and enthusing other individuals about
the subject, you will make new discoveries which further your own
knowledge and ideas.

While the usual image of a teacher is of a grown-up standing in
front of a classroom of children, it should be remembered that
teaching can also mean one-to-one sessions, private lessons such as
musical instrument tuition, further education, higher education,
evening classes and even working as a teacher/trainer in a corporate
environment. The latter could mean tutoring individuals in specific
work processes, or helping to develop general management skills.

Main industry trends

In recent years the government has worked hard to make entrance
into the teaching profession more attractive to graduates. There are
now a number of flexible training/entrance courses and a plethora of
financial incentives, particularly around subjects where there is a
great demand for teachers. In spite of these incentives, the public
sector education system still does not give as healthy remuneration as

is possible through the private sector, in corporate education or even through the delivery of personal tuition.

Classroom teaching to help pupils reach national standards can be extremely challenging and rewarding, with or without you taking on extracurricular activities (putting on performances, running after-school clubs etc). At the same time, the increased emphasis on teaching the National Curriculum has brought extra pressure to bear on teaching staff and to some extent has reduced their freedom to teach. For good teachers, however, the opportunities are there to make a significant contribution to the management and life of a school, thereby playing a crucial part in the life of all youngsters in an entire community.

The Internet is radically changing the way subjects are taught, the way learning is shared around companies, industries and within education institutions. On the one hand, the Internet provides a vast resource for students of all ages to access knowledge and carry out their own research, but there is also the temptation to download material which they may claim is their own response to an assignment. Taken too far, this can be detrimental to the individual's education – proving that they are adept at using the Google search engine rather than understanding their subject.

The Internet and related communications technology can provide a useful infrastructure for education purposes. Tele-conferencing enables students in one part of the world to view live images of procedures in another part of the world – whether this be a lecture or a practical demonstration of equipment or processes. Distance learning and entire e-learning packages can be created and put online for students to access and use at a time that best suits them individually.

Competition throughout every part of business means that employees need to keep their skills finely honed and up to date. Business is increasingly looking to professional trainers to find ways of making sure that their employees' skills are at the highest level at all times.

Ways into the workplace

The Teacher Training Agency publishes all information necessary for graduates – and undergraduates who are seeking to enter the teaching profession. Their Web site includes details of the financial incentives (including £6000 training bursary, and the possibility of £4000 'golden hellos' for appropriate trainees) as well as the Fast Track scheme which identifies qualified applicants who can be developed for leadership positions in the profession within five or six years.

PGCE qualifications are the traditional way into the profession; these last a year and include 2–3 placements in the classroom. Alternatively, you may take a School Centred Initial Teacher Training course (SCITT) which, as its name suggests, is a school-based full-time training scheme. Go to www.gttr.ac.uk (The Graduate Teacher Training Registry) for more information or call 01242 544788.

Teachers in the further and higher education sector do not necessarily need a teaching qualification but will need a very good degree in their subject area. These tutors tend to find their way into the profession via research work or postgraduate study which attaches them to an education establishment. Once here, students may find that they are allocated teaching responsibilities as part of their timetable within their department. This work is paid and will cover a subject of which they will already have full knowledge from undergraduate study. As time goes by, the amount and standard of this work can increase. When you achieve your postgraduate qualification – especially if it is a research-based qualification – you will be able to apply for more challenging and financially remunerating teaching posts. If you have gained a PhD or doctorate in your subject you will be able to apply for the highest positions within university faculties and departments.

In some areas of higher education – particularly in research-based posts – teaching can be regarded as secondary to the demands of your job. However, in recent years the importance of departmental performance has meant that the workload and scrutiny under which lecturers and tutors operate and teach have risen substantially.

As a private teacher you do not require any official qualification to recognize your ability to teach, but you do need a vocational qualification in your field. You may be an excellent pianist but unless you have some recognition from an awards body you are unlikely to attract students. You should have proof of qualifications from a relevant examination board – such as the London Academy of Music and Dramatic Arts. Private teachers and peripatetic teachers – those who travel from location to location (sometimes school to school) – will only gain and maintain their livelihood through reputation. That means being popular with students and getting them through their exams.

The world of corporate training splits roughly into two. You can either be an in-house trainer – part of the human resources/personnel function who are responsible for ensuring the skills of the workforce are up to the challenge of the jobs they are required to do, or you could be an independent specialist trainer, working for an external company of consultants, called upon by a variety of clients for your specialist skills.

It should be clear that teaching adults is a very different proposition from children – there are pros and cons of both student groups. Adults tend to be less flexible and more demanding in terms of needing a reason to take on board new skills. They may be set in their ways and even regard the assimilation of new skills as a threat to their current working life. For this reason, you may find teaching at this level a greater challenge than a class of six-year-olds.

The world of corporate learning can command extremely high fees, especially if you are able to specialize in your subject to the point of achieving 'guru' status. Once you've done this, you can secure lucrative publishing deals, and charge immense sums for consultancy work or for making presentations and personal appearances.

Professional bodies offering jobs, information and further education

TeachFirst – a scheme which places qualified graduates into paid teaching positions for two years before they go into business: www.teachfirst.co.uk; Teach First, 1 Hobhouse Court, Suffolk Street, London SW1Y 4HH; Tel: 020 76651451.

London Academy of Music and Dramatic Arts
LAMDA, 155 Talgarth Road, London W14 9DE;
Tel: 020 7373 9883; www.lamda.org.uk.

DfES Student Support line: 0900 7319133.
Teaching Information Line: 0845 6000991.

Chartered Institute of Personnel and Development
CIPD House, Camp Road, Wimbledon, London SW19 4UX;
Tel: 020 8971 9000; www.peoplemanagement.co.uk.
Separate section for trainers, professional body for corporate development.

TrainingZone – Institute of Continuing Professional Development
100 Victoria Street, Bristol BS1 6HZ; Tel: 0117 915 9600.
Online resource for news and training issues.

The public sector

For a long time viewed as second to working in the private sector, public sector employment has suffered principally from levels of remuneration rather than the challenge and career potential offered to graduates. Indeed, working directly to improve the overall running of the country – whether through a national directorate or a local government organization – holds a unique challenge in terms of the scale of work required and the influence you can have over public life.

While remaining politically independent, public service work does come under a lot of pressure from the government to perform and to deliver the improvements they have been elected to deliver. The public service is fast outstripping its old 'inefficient' image and embracing new technologies and processes in order to give more value for money to the public who pay for these services.

Main industry trends

The public sector is driving hard towards a concept called 'joined-up government'. The idea here is to bring diverse parts of government operation closer together and to reduce bureaucracy. For example, rather than diverse parts of a local government authority collecting and recording information on a customer – housing benefit, council tax, social services etc – that information should be collected only once and shared around the organization. In the criminal justice sector, details of criminal activities could also be recorded only once and used to provide a clear pathway from the police officer working on a case through to prosecution of the suspect, rather than requiring the repeated collection of evidence and statements from witnesses and victims as a case proceeds to the courts.

In some cases the streamlining of government processes has meant re-engineering entire departments – changing the way work is carried out and altering the responsibilities and job descriptions of employees. In other cases there has been extensive use of IT and communications technology, bringing diverse areas of the public sector closer together. Indeed, parts of the public sector – such as the NHS – are facing massive changes in their technology use and huge investment in new systems. Being able to deliver an effective service while implementing new systems is just one challenge that public sector professionals will face over the next few years.

As part of this change in the public service, the private sector has been invited to get involved on an unprecedented scale. Consultants, IT companies, construction businesses and recruitment services have been brought in to bring better services at a more cost-efficient price to the sector. It is always difficult to adapt to working with external parties but when these companies are intended to play a permanent or long-term role in service provision it takes a high level of management skill to ensure that working relationships are effective and deliver the required results. There have been many examples where such arrangements have failed to perform as expected, and each time these failures have occurred they have been greeted with dismay and scandal by the press and media, regardless of the reason for that failure.

In recent years there has been a far greater level of accountability brought to operations and processes in the public sector. There are new methods of measuring performance – school league tables, scoring systems for hospitals and health organizations, and even continuous professional assessment (CPA) for local government authorities. All of these are intended to ensure that the public sector operates in an atmosphere of continuous improvement and delivers value for money to the people it serves. At the same time, all of these initiatives bring extra pressure to bear on the people working in the public sector since the public's expectation of services continually rises.

Whereas it used to be the case that professionals worked either in the public sector or the private sector, there is now far more crossover of staff between the two. A number of senior-level professionals have entered the public sector following a career in industry, managing processes and people within large organizations. The commercial knowledge held by the private sector is now perceived as more relevant to the public sector where the people they serve are increasingly seen as their customers. As a result, successful graduates will need strong commercial skills to help their organizations meet the unlimited demands of their customers despite the limited resources available to them.

Ways into the workplace

While it is possible to move around various positions in the public sector, it is important to have some idea of the type of work you want to do or the type of organization where you want to work. There are different challenges available to managers in the health service compared with managers who are working for local government authorities. Similarly, the work available within a single local authority can be extremely diverse, ranging from social services to the education department to the maintenance of parks and public spaces.

Alternatively, you may wish to work within a central government department such as the Department for Education and Skills or the Department for Trade and Industry. At this level, graduates can be fast-tracked into high-ranking positions as analysts, economists and researchers. They may be called upon to create and assess government policy – to determine the overall effects of certain initiatives, to cost out their likely financial cost and speculate on their probable impact. Again, employment can range from something like this in policy and research to press office duties and communication management – perhaps even designing initiatives to explain to the public what new initiatives mean and how they will be implemented.

Promotion within the public service is very much dependent on experience and performance, although employment does bring a well-structured rewards package and graded increases in pay. At a time when the government is seeking to encourage flexible working and reduce working hours across the UK's population, public sector workers should be among the first to experience these changes to working patterns.

Professional bodies offering jobs, information and further education

Much recruitment for the public sector is carried out by:
Capita RAS
Innovation Court, New Street, Basingstoke, Hampshire RG21 7JB;
Tel: 01256 869555; www.rasnet.co.uk.

Employment opportunities are also advertised and accessible through public sector Web sites. For a complete directory of such sites try: www.tagish.co.uk/Links/.
For further recruitment opportunities, contact your local government authority direct.

Retail

Many people who enjoy the shopping experience will be pleased to find that they can make an enjoyable and lucrative career within the industry itself, not just admiring the products on the shelf but deciding what products should be on those shelves, how they should be presented and even determining the price and profit made each time one of those products is bought.

The role of store manager may be the most immediate position associated with this area of work, but this is more of a transitory role for graduates. They may pass through the job in order to gain a general view of the retail organization – how it interfaces with customers – before heading for a more senior position within another part of the company operation. This could include working in buying, finance, supply, systems, human resources or marketing.

Main industry trends

Retail has become a multi-channel operation, with digital television and the Internet offering new, international shopping options which compete with more conventional methods such as catalogue shopping and home delivery. Retail organizations are looking to maximize the number and type of outlets they have, bearing in mind that a Web-site-driven sale will cost less in overheads than a sale in a conventional store where staff and shop costs are incurred. These different types of outlets are sometimes referred to as bricks, flicks and clicks (built shops, catalogues and Web sites respectively).

As retail companies explore new methods of reaching the public and selling goods, careful attention is paid to branding in order to ensure that each selling route will appeal to the appropriate customers. Customers who use the Internet in order to source discounted items will be happy with a very basic site, whereas a youth-oriented brand or a more upmarket store will need a more stylish and complex Web site to attract business.

Discount stores have proliferated in recent years, bringing increased competition to an already competitive industry. The pressure is on for workers in the merchandising/buyer functions to find product sources which offer quality goods at marked-down prices.

Regardless of Internet use, retail is a global industry. Not only can products be sourced from around the world and imported at a cheaper price than if they were produced in the UK, but some items can be made more efficiently by sourcing components from diverse factories around the world, assembling and packaging them at another location.

Retail is as much about image as it is about providing customer value. Marketing staff need to be sure that the products on offer tie in with the store image and appeal directly to the store's customers. Unless a company competes on price alone – becoming a pure discount store – it is the image and the label that will gain and keep customers. At the same time, the globalization of manufacturing has resulted in a significant number of customers becoming concerned about the exploitation of labour in the developing world. Fair trade and ethically produced goods have a strong and growing market.

The fortunes of retail companies are frequently regarded as a marker of wider economic health in the UK. If company profits are high, consumer spending is high and this has implications for the amount of money flowing around the economy. If sales are low, many economists immediately start talking about a global economic downturn.

Ways into the workplace

The retail industry has a strong reputation for graduate training schemes. These courses can be intensive and challenging but they get you using your skills in a management context almost as soon as you start. Very often graduates will be allocated a mentor or supervisor for their first year who will offer support and guidance as they progress.

Graduate schemes will include shop floor experience – often from every point of view – so you may find yourself operating the tills one week, stacking shelves and managing the flow of stock through the warehouse the next. In this way you will receive a full understanding of exactly what the operation is about – unless you have this kind of grounding it is unlikely that you will understand how your work in other areas of the company contributes to the store itself.

Having completed your graduate induction scheme, you can either stay on the shop floor side of operations – assuming responsibility for greater numbers of stores within an increasing geographical area – or take your skills to the back-office arena. A job such as merchandising or buying can include international travel since you will be tasked with finding new product ranges to tie in with each new season and to ensure that these items can be sourced in a way that profits the company. This area of retail operates at least three months ahead of the rest of the company – sometimes as much as six months or a year ahead – so while the shop may be selling winter clothes, the buyers are already striking deals for the summer range.

Managing supply chains and systems is increasingly important as technology has offered ways to increase communications across the company as well as between customer and retail outlet. Technology has also provided the ability to automate stock management so as soon as an item passes through the checkout, the sale is recorded and a replacement item ordered. Identifying ways to increase efficiency in the order and delivery of products – making sure that products arrive on the shelf just when they are required – is key to maximizing the profits of a retail organization.

Professional bodies offering jobs, information and further education

Consortium of Retail Teaching Companies
c/o Marks and Spencer, Michael House, Baker Street, London W1X 3LB; www.cortco.co.uk/index.htm.
Promotes graduate opportunities in retail and includes links to all major retail companies.

British Retail Consortium
Second Floor, 21 Dartmouth Street, London SW1H 9BP;
Tel: 020 7647 1500; www.brc.org.uk.
Industry body representing retail companies.

Chartered Institute of Purchasing and Supply
Education Department, Easton House, Easton on the Hill, Stamford, Lincolnshire PE9 3NZ; Tel: 01780 756777; www.cips.org.
Professional body and accreditation for professionals in buying and merchandising roles.

Chartered Institute of Management Accountants
26 Chapter Street, London SW1P 4NP; Tel: 020 7663 5441;
www.cimaglobal.com.
Offers professional training and recognition for accountants.

Information technology

There can be little doubt that as a graduate, whatever you do, sooner or later there will be a computer attached to your working life. Whether you are simply typing up worksheets for a tutorial that you are leading or trying to create code to support a computer game, IT skills are intrinsic to a successful career. For those intending to make a career within the information technology sector there are two paths to consider. First, you can be a specialist in the use of IT – someone who is aware of the programs and applications available on the market and who can use these in the most efficient way for their employer. The second path is to be at the cutting edge of the technology itself – writing code and programs for games or business use, domestic applications or commercial Web sites.

In both cases it is imperative that you keep yourself informed of the latest technologies in development and on the market. Technology is moving forward at a rapid pace, with faster and more efficient machines being created almost every day. Your success may be entirely bound up with up-to-date knowledge of IT, the constant danger being that if you lose track of its progress, you could be regarded as someone with last year's knowledge and talent.

Main industry trends

While international IT organizations fight over the main commercial markets, there are diverse opportunities for small and medium-sized firms. The IT world is now so vast that there is a constant need for specialisms within the use of applications and within specific industries. If you intend to use your IT skills within a specific industry, you will need to understand that industry inside out. You may need to undergo further study in order to get to know your marketplace. Simply offering a generic solution may not satisfy your customer. Indeed, a database application for use in a domestic appliances reseller company is not going to be appropriate for a health sector organization.

Information technology is a global business. Thanks to good educational institutions and cheap labour in other parts of the world, there are many examples where organizations find it more cost-effective to outsource programming development outside the UK rather than employing IT professionals here. This practice drives up the levels of skills required by UK IT professionals. They can only secure work through providing extra-value services – work that essentially cannot be sourced or carried out anywhere else in the world.

There may be the perception that IT is all about getting the next best product, program or system to market, but there is also substantial work to be done in the management of old or legacy systems. As technological progress continues, many large customer service oriented organizations find that the equipment they use for their everyday work becomes obsolete or impossible to use alongside the most recent technologies. Work is therefore required to create interfaces between old and new systems. This integration work is particularly relevant in the public sector where investment in IT can lag behind the private sector. Moreover, by integrating systems in this way, organizations can gain maximum value from their technology – using it alongside new solutions rather than having to junk the whole lot and invest from scratch.

Today, a company or organization without a Web site is missing out on a huge opportunity for gaining extra interest and customers for their services. While basic Web-site creation is not rocket science, designing a Web page that is attractive and promotes interaction between visitor and organization is a highly regarded skill and there are no end of companies who offer Web hosting and development services. Moreover, the Internet has become a new marketplace for retail organizations, bringing with it new challenges for security in the automation of transactions. Graduates can look forward to a long and lucrative career if they are able to contribute to this area of commerce.

The market for dedicated game-playing consoles as well as PC and Internet-based games has skyrocketed over the past 10 years. The demand for more realistic graphics, more involving games and a more detailed level of interaction offers all sorts of opportunities for those working in technology – whether they be programmers charged with creating realistic on-screen environments or games writers trying to search out new subjects, angles and approaches to creating addictive games. Graduates who are already into the games market can find themselves contributing to the next stage in gaming if they combine market knowledge with the right technical skills.

Ways into the workplace

Some large IT companies run graduate training schemes and look to employ a number of graduates each year. Competition for such positions is fierce and the rewards high, and while the number of recruits taken on varies from year to year, reflecting market and company confidence, graduates who take this route can be certain of a good start to their career. Such schemes will cover all areas of IT business – from the domestic applications market to business consulting and integration work – with a larger number of opportunities tending to lie in business-to-business work.

With the right skills it is possible to approach individual IT companies – be they Web design agencies, game creators or even manufacturing companies – and offer your skills without waiting for a recruitment advert to appear. It may be that you are knocked back, but IT companies will always be on the lookout for skilled workers to contribute to a variety of projects, not all of which will be advertised or disclosed to the world in general.

It is also possible to establish yourself as a freelance IT worker in the industry. Wherever you end up, you are likely to be assigned to a project with a strict delivery deadline and therefore be expected to move on once your work on that project is completed. If you are with a major employer their HR department may well be responsible for directing you to a new project offering new challenges and so on. You may find as you proceed through your career that you become more involved in project management – ensuring that certain targets are hit in terms of performance and delivery deadlines – rather than doing the programming or technical work yourself. If you are a freelance worker you will be in charge of your own career development, so you will need to create a good network of contacts to ensure that you are in demand and can use your skills in a lucrative and fulfilling way.

Alternatively, if you want to find your way into a systems management position, you will need to track down vacancies within the IT departments of employers. You may find a position at IT administration level within a local government organization or within the IT department of a retail company, for example. At entry level you will be expected to monitor system performance and ensure that the system is effectively maintained. Getting to know the job at this level means that you will have a good background for promotion, ultimately designing and implementing systems yourself.

Professional bodies offering jobs, information and further education

Institute for the Management of Information Services
5 Kingfisher House, New Mill Road, Orpington, Kent BR5 3QG;
Tel: 0700 0023456; www.imis.org.uk.
Professional recognition body with training and career support.

Institution of Analysts and Programmers (IAP)
Charles House, 36 Culmington Road, London W13 9NH;
Tel: 020 8567 2118; www.iap.org.uk.
Continuous professional development resources plus careers support.

Intellect
Russell Square House, 10–12 Russell Square, London WC1B 5EE;
Tel: 020 7331 2000; www.cssa.co.uk.
Trade body representing computing industry, includes access to training and day courses.

British Computer Society
1 Sanford Street, Swindon, Wiltshire SN1 1HJ; Tel: 01793 417417;
www1.bcs.org.uk.
Industry news and comment, professional qualifications and career guidance.

Police and armed forces

The police and armed forces provide one of the most challenging environments in which anyone can work. While not every job means working at the front line, the focus of the work is there – to assess risks and to protect the lives of the people you serve. Every other discipline in these organizations must work to ensure that frontline workers can do their jobs efficiently and effectively.

The police have arguably the most visible job in the UK. It is a role dogged by controversy – fierce national and local arguments have been triggered by the work and attitude of the police – and there is a political context to the work as well, with successive governments making promises to the public about cutting the level of crime and disorder, altering the priorities and powers of the police to fulfil these promises. And even when the crime figures fall – which they have in some areas over recent years – the force still has to address the perception of the public that crime continues to rise.

The armed services – comprising the Royal Navy, Royal Air Force and the British Army – have an international scope in their duties. There are overseas postings and roles as peacekeeping forces or even providing health and welfare support to areas affected by conflict. In other words, working for the armed forces does not mean that you contribute nothing unless the country goes to war.

Each part of the armed forces is backed by further operation and support staff at the Ministry of Defence. While the primary purpose of the forces may be to provide security for the UK, there are countless other roles within these services to do with functions as diverse as medical treatment and technology (IT as well as other gadgetry). Given the environment in which these organizations perform, the armed forces tend to be at the cutting edge of research and development in technology. New advances in military equip-ment can sometimes find applications in civilian, peacetime life.

Main industry trends

The police, along with the rest of the legal system, are facing a great period of change, with increased technology use and changes in managerial structure affecting their day-to-day job. Systems such as global satellite positioning and enhanced radio communica-tions all help to maximize the time that officers can spend on the beat and minimize the time spent on administrative tasks. There is an increased used of electronic links between each of the UK's police forces to gather information and perform searches for suspects nation-wide. There is also increased use of tech-nology for the presentation and collection of evidence in a case. The Internet is also enabling petty and low-priority crimes to be reported and recorded online rather than taking up an officer's time.

Of course, the Internet has also created another place where criminal activities can occur. Not only are child pornography networks a relatively new and serious issue, but also criminals can use Web sites for the purposes of fraud and deception as well as communicating with each other. These new crimes require constant vigilance and an ever-evolving approach to criminal investigation.

As with many other areas of the public sector, the police service could do with more resources and sometimes it is argued that there is insufficient funding to provide officers and operational staff with the support they need. Regardless of future levels of investment, as an officer, an inspector or senior manager within the force, you are likely to experience frustration with insufficient resources.

The Royal Navy, Royal Air Force and British Army do not work purely on UK-focused activities. They are often to be found working alongside other international agencies and forces, peacekeeping in some parts of the world, delivering aid to other countries and playing a crucial part when a show of force is required.

The forces – in particular the British Army – have a seemingly endless array of job opportunities. Once in the Army, it is possible to train in specialisms ranging from dog handler to farrier. Alternatively, you can enter the army as a musician – you still get all the rigorous military training – or as a nurse or other medical staff.

While the size of the armed forces has diminished over the past 20 years or so, it is still one of the largest employers in the UK and continues to offer demanding, internationally based graduate-level careers. There is a clear promotional and development path for officers, and as a graduate recruit you should reach the level of Lieutenant Commander (a middle management position) in 5–7 years.

Positions within the civil service and within the research and development arm of the MOD (the Defence Evaluation and Research Agency, or DERA) are also influenced by the international perspective of the department's work. No matter what your discipline, you are unlikely to be tied to the same desk in the same city or country for very long.

Ways into the workplace

Applications for both the police and the armed services are fairly structured via the local police services or local armed forces careers offices. As a graduate you may be able to get onto a Fast Stream course (see www.faststream.gov.uk) within the civil service, a High Potential Development Scheme or the Accelerated Promotion Scheme for Graduates in the police force. Alternatively, you may be able to enter the armed services at an officer level rather than a lower rank.

Whatever your entrance point, you will be subjected to standard tests and to a rigorous training process. The full course for police officers lasts around two years and comprises placements and on-the-job work at all levels in the service. This means that even if you want to specialize in CID or forensic work you will still have the experience and knowledge of what it's like to work on the beat.

Unsurprisingly, the armed forces provide a very physical training programme for new entrants. You will see many different areas of operations before working towards your particular area of expertise. In this case, however, you may find that each new posting takes you to a different part of the world rather than to a different area of the UK.

Professional bodies offering jobs, information and further education

www.policecouldyou.co.uk.
Web site with information and challenges for those considering entering the police force.

Accelerated Promotion Scheme for Graduates
Police Graduate Liaison Officer, Room 556, Home Office,
50 Queen Anne's Gate, London SW1H 9AT;
www.police.uk/recruitment.asp.

The Royal Navy
www.royal-navy.mod.uk.
Includes list of local Officer Career Liaison Centres:
www.royal-navy.mod.uk/static/pages/3379.html.

London Officer Career Liaison Centre: 1a Iverna Gardens, Kensington, London W8 6TN; Tel: 020 7938 4646.

The British Army
www.army.mod.uk/careers/index.htm.

Also: www.armyjobs.co.uk – for a searchable database of current
opportunities.
Unit 16, Westminster Court, Hipley Street, Old Woking, Surrey
GU22 9LQ; Tel: 08700 0131200.

Royal Air Force
www.rafcareers.com.
List of nearest recruitment centres at:
www.rafcareers.com/html/goforit/afco.html.

AFCO (RAF) London
453 The Strand, London WCR2 0RG; and Room G146,
St Christopher House, 90–114 Southwark Street, London SE1 0TD;
Tel: 020 7305 4278.

Civil service and Fast Stream schemes recruited by:
Capita RAS
Innovation Court, New Street, Basingstoke, Hampshire RG21 7JB;
Tel: 01256 383683; www.faststream.gov.uk.

Science and technology

The field of science and technology can be rewarding both financially and in terms of job satisfaction. It can also be one of the most
frustrating and unrecognized areas of work. The difference between
these two employment states is to do with the sector in which you
operate as a scientist and who your employer is. If, for example, you
find yourself working as a geologist in the research department of a
fuel company, or a chemist within a multinational pharmaceutical
company, the chances are that you will be well resourced and
supported in the work you do – discovering and developing
programmes to locate and extract fossil fuels or concocting new
drugs to meet the needs of patients. If, on the other hand, you are
attached to a research programme funded primarily by the public

sector, you may find your work constantly compromised by funding issues. Indeed, you may find that your working life is as dedicated to finding new sources of income and making appropriate applications as it is to actually carrying out the research.

Whatever your field, as a scientist or technology professional you will be working at the cutting edge of your profession. You will be reviewing current practice and pushing back the boundaries of knowledge, working towards the creation of new and lucrative products and procedures which will contribute to a better lifestyle for the population in general.

Main industry trends

Research and development is the most expensive activity any company can carry out. In the pharmaceutical industry, it is recognized that new drugs must sell extensively and command a reasonably high market price in order to recoup these expenses. Similarly, the cost of finding new fuel and energy resources or developing new electronic technology must always deliver a significant benefit for commercial organizations. To this extent you may find research work limited or at least channelled towards projects regarded as more likely to provide a healthy payback.

The science and technology industry is a worldwide one and thanks to information technology and increased communications it is now possible to link the resources and knowledge of scientists from around the world in order to focus on advances. Science and technology companies tend to be multinational operations with markets in all parts of the world. This scale of operation gives them a stable base from which to operate and it gives you an internationally based career.

Scientists and technologists usually work on a project-by-project basis. They also may be attached to specific operations in order to monitor and direct activities, rather than simply developing new processes. For example, they may be employed to troubleshoot problems in a manufacturing scenario – perhaps ensuring that large-scale factories still produce the same quality product as was created within a smaller set-up or even the laboratory setting.

While you may have your work cut out convincing funding bodies that your work is worthwhile, there is also some scepticism within the general public as to what precisely scientists and technologists do. On the one hand there is controversy when a scientist suggests a new technology or technique which generates concern among the press and public – experimentation on human genes, for example. There is also outcry when scientists appear to have spent resources on a project which results in an obvious or very low value result.

Ways into the workplace

As mentioned above, scientists and technology workers operate in a wide range of industry sectors, and therefore the number and type of opportunities available to graduates are diverse. A food technologist, hoping for a job in food science (anything from research into nutrition to the design of convenience/ready-to-eat meals) will have to take a radically different approach from someone working in the cosmetics industry. Even in the cosmetics industry there is now a clear split between the 'ethical' producers who use only naturally occurring materials and do not test products on animals and those organizations that use chemicals and do still test on animals.

You should identify the part of industry you hope to work for and find a relevant project in which to get involved. Your first work may seem very trivial – perhaps recording and collating test results, for example, but even this role is important to do accurately and coherently and will give you an insight into the way of working within your employer and industry. Alternatively, you may find that you are able to carry out research as part of your continuing academic career. You may know of a scientific department which already has good links with a funding source – whether that source is within industry or the public sector. You may be able to set up your own scientific programme of research which keys into the needs and work of other organizations or companies.

Research work falls under two headings: pure research and applied research. The former is carried out as a general activity – to further scientific knowledge in a particular area. The second is geared to a specific need within an organization or company.

Some scientific work directly interfaces with the public. Information such as the weather forecast comes from meteorologists at the Meteorological Office, a publicly funded organization which provides information to many organizations affected by the weather, including the armed forces, who need to take the elements into account when planning their manoeuvres.

Scientific and technology roles demand a level of interaction with people outside the profession, so to be truly employable you need to speak the language of the professional in that sector as well as the language of the scientist. You may find yourself working alongside structural engineers in determining the strength of a particular material used in construction. You may be required to determine the all-round performance of a plastic material used in the home environment. Is the material suitable and safe for the application intended? Scientists are often used as part of the Quality Assurance programme within manufacturing systems to prove the robust nature of a product or to establish the expected life span of a product.

In many ways, science and technology provide the innovative capacity of an economy. Research enables companies and organizations to progress with their activities and find new markets and benefits for their customers. The profession will always be essential, but it is closely linked to the economic fortune of the country – therefore, if spending and profits fall, the amount of money available for future development is likely to be cut as well.

Professional bodies offering jobs, information and further education

Association of Clinical Research in the Pharmaceutical Industry (ACRPI)
PO Box 1208, Maidenhead, Berkshire SL6 3GD; Tel: 01628 829900; www.acrpi.com.
Offers continual professional development, vacancies and a section for freelance researchers.

Association of British Pharmaceutical Industry
12 Whitehall, London SW1A 2DY; Tel: 020 7930 3477; www.abpi.org.uk.

Trade association for pharmaceutical companies. Includes links to careers site: www.abpi-careers.org.uk.

Royal Society of Chemistry
Burlington House, Piccadilly, London W1J 0BA; Tel: 020 7437 8656; www.chemsoc.ce.com.
Information on chemistry industry and a separate skills centre area for professional development.

Institute of Food Science and Technology
5 Cambridge Court, 210 Shepherd's Bush Road, London W6 7NJ; Tel: 020 7603 6316; www.easynet.co.uk/ifst/.
Professional recognition and continuous professional development resources.

Association of Clinical Biochemists
130–132 Tooley Street, London SE1 2TU; Tel: 020 7403 8001; www.acb.org.uk.
Training and professional recognition body.

British Geological Survey
Kingsley Dunham Centre, Keyworth, Nottingham NG12 5GG; Tel: 0115 9363100; www.bgs.ac.uk.

Society of Petroleum Engineers
4th Floor, Empire House, 175 Piccadilly, London W1J 9EN; Tel: 020 7408 4466; www.spe.org.
Links, information and further training within the petroleum industry.

Engineering Council (UK)
10 Maltravers Street, London WC2R 3ER; Tel: 020 7240 7891; www.engc.org.uk.
Diploma-awarding body, careers and job links.

Institute of Materials, Minerals and Mining
1 Carlton House Terrace, London SW1Y 5DB; Tel: 020 74517300; www.iom3.org.
Runs the IOM Academy offering further training and professional recognition.

Agriculture

The provision of food within the UK is an evolving and challenging business. Aside from the particular hardships and ordeals faced by the farming community over the past few years, the industry itself is facing major changes while all the time trying to provide food at a cost-effective price. The fact is that there are so many influences which can affect food production in the UK – everything from weather to diet scares – that securing a reliable income from working in the industry is by no means guaranteed.

That said, the challenge falls to qualified graduates in the sector to develop and implement new and efficient ways of managing food resources. Farm management is only one way of contributing to this process, since each farm relies on the provision of seeds, pesticides and machinery to harvest the maximum return from the soil. At the same time, concerns over the use of GM technology and the rise in popularity of organic produce have led to what used to be a niche market becoming a significant business opportunity. Increasingly health-conscious consumers believe that organic produce is key to a good diet – be it organic vegetables or animal products.

Main industry trends

In recent years the farming industry has had to cope with Foot and Mouth, BSE ('mad cow disease') and the advent of genetically modi-fied crops. The first two of these have thrown a negative light on the treatment and management of animals. Regardless of the origin of Foot and Mouth, the conditions in which animals were kept and transported contributed to the scale of the epidemic. BSE has been traced back to the practice of feeding animals with feed that had animal products in it – effectively turning these herbivores into canni-bals. GM crops, at one time thought to be the answer to global food shortages, has suffered from a bad press and less than enthusiastic responses from the food industry in general. Rather than being regarded as a way of maximizing yield from a patch of land, these crops are seen as 'Frankenstein' produce, at odds with nature, the long-term effects of which are unknown and perhaps damaging to the health of humans.

There is also substantial change occurring to the finance and support received by the farming community. The Common Agricultural Policy – the European trade agreement which supports farmers through supplements and guaranteed prices – is considered to be far too expensive to maintain and effectively removes the influence of the free market on the sector. However this is resolved, the UK farming population will need to reassess the way they operate and even change the crops they grow in order to survive.

The rise of organic produce is welcome but it takes time for a plot of land to be recognized as organic – this is the time it takes for the artificial pesticides and nutrients to leave the soil. Even then, increased competition from foreign producers can compromise the return made by farmers on their produce.

It has been suggested that the role of farmers in the future should be given a different emphasis – away from food producer and towards a 'caretaker of the land' role. In this way, the farming community could be rewarded for the maintenance of a diverse landscape, rather than allowing the business/profit motive to dictate a policy of maximizing crop production at the cost of the long-term well-being of the countryside.

All these influences impact throughout the agricultural industry – affecting not only the farmers themselves but their support networks and the people to whom they contract work. There are many agriculturally based companies offering equipment, pesticides and fertilizers that help farmers in their work. There are also transport companies, rendering plants and even veterinary surgeons who depend on the farming industry for their livelihood. Substantial changes to farmers' lives – and even changes to the attitude of the public towards the food they produce – have already been seen to have a massive knock-on effect to other parts of the industry and across entire communities.

Ways into the workplace

Traditionally, farm management and ownership has been a family affair, with responsibility being transferred along with skills and resources down each new generation. This is still overwhelmingly the case, leaving those outside the farming community waiting for opportunities within farms to arise as and when farmers decide they need extra help. Very often this help will be seasonal – with peaks occurring according to the type of agricultural activities they are engaged in. The requirement for extra hands at lambing time, for example, is different from the demand experienced when arable farmers hit their harvest.

For the graduate, a more common way in will be through one of the farming support companies – a fertilizer company or agricultural consultancy. In the first of these examples, opportunities may exist for new graduates in selling or representative roles. The function here is to visit farmers on site, assess whether they would be good customers for the company's product and organize contracts and deliveries with the farmer. Not all farms will be suitable customers for particular pesticides or fertilizers – the expense of investing in such products can outstrip any additional return experienced by the farmer.

Consultants are increasingly finding a role in all areas of farming – including the organic sector. Here, qualified experts can be called into farms to offer advice on particular aspects of their work or to give an overall view and audit of a farm's operation. They may need to suggest ways in which the land can be better used – a change of crops or extension of planting. They may need to draw up a programme of how to progress to becoming an organic operation or draw up a clear business plan for the farmer to move towards organic production.

Graduates may also be involved in the research and development side of crops. This may not always mean managing a GM crop site – there can also be work in examining the performance of different types of arable crops, deciding whether they may be more suitable for UK land and climate.

Agricultural students may carry out work with a wider environmental remit, advising on complementary planting – where one crop benefits from the close proximity of another – or ensuring that all work on the landscape is environmentally friendly and will not have long-term negative effects. Such work is common within public sector organizations, many of which operate under the auspices of the Department for the Environment, Food and Rural Affairs (DEFRA).

Professional bodies offering jobs, information and further education

Agriculture Development and Advisory Centre
ADAS, Wolverhampton HQ, Woodthorne, Wergs Road,
Wolverhampton WV6 8TQ; Tel: 01902 754190; www.adas.co.uk.
Carries out research and consultation within the agricultural industry.

Department for the Environment, Food and Rural Affairs
Personnel, Management and Development Division, Room 227,
Nobel House, 17 Smith Square, London SW1 2HH;
Tel: 020 7238 5733; www.defra.gov.uk.
Links to recruitment site, publications and other government agencies.

Association of Independent Crop Consultants
Agriculture House, Station Road, Liss, Hampshire GU33 7AR;
Tel: 01730 895354; www.aicc.org.uk.
Recognizes independent professionals working in crop management
– ie consultants who do not work for one particular crop manufacturer.

Institute of Agricultural Engineers
West End Road, Silsoe, Bedford MK45 4DU; Tel: 01525 861096;
www.iagre.org.
Courses and continuous professional development for all management-level workers in land-based resources.

Soil Association
Bristol House, 40–56 Victoria Street, Bristol BS1 6BY;
Tel: 0117 9290661; www.soilassociation.org.
Official recognition body for organic produce; offers information on organic management and work.

Velcourt Farm Management
Melbury Sampford, Dorchester, Dorset BT2 0LF; Tel: 01935 83739;
www.velcourt.co.uk.
Company providing farming management professionals for tenant and owner farmers.

European site for the Common Agricultural Policy:
http://europa.eu.int/comm/agriculture/index_en.htm.

Leisure and tourism

Leisure and tourism account for a significant amount of UK consumer spending. Working in the leisure and tourism sector means being responsible for providing all UK employees with a chance to break away from their working lives, to recuperate, rejuvenate and chill out before going back to their job. There are a wide variety of industries and employment opportunities included in this area. There are leisure centres such as sports centres, swimming pools, or theme parks such as Alton Towers or Thorpe Park. Leisure activities can also include technology areas such as computers and the production of dedicated games consoles.

While UK tourism offers opportunities for graduates to work in this country, there are many opportunities for foreign travel and graduates are ideally placed to take on the more responsible kind of holiday rep work. Meanwhile, on the retail side of the tourism industry, well-travelled graduates can exploit opportunities in 'destination management', especially with the growing market for the more adventurous traveller. It should be noted, however, that in this area advances in technology are having an impact. Customers can now buy their holiday products direct from the providers and secure significant discounts by purchasing via the Internet.

Main industry trends

Recent world events have demonstrated how the tourism sector is sensitive to public opinion, with travel plans being significantly affected by international relationships and occurrences. In the UK, Foot and Mouth followed by the tragedy of 11 September 2001 and the continued threat of terrorism has impacted negatively on the number of foreign tourists coming to the country. However, while terrorist attacks may have checked the growth in international travel, there remains a healthy demand for increasingly 'out the way' and 'adventurous' destinations, particularly among the younger age group.

Internet technology is impacting on the operation of 'destination management' (travel agencies and related services). Technology is effectively 'unpacking' the package holiday, enabling the users to select separate elements of their holiday as they require. This, together with increased use of online booking, is affecting the number and type of jobs in this area. At the same time, hotel chains and holiday operators are creating new alliances and merging to realize economies of scale. Consequently, there are fewer but larger organizations across the sector.

Meanwhile, interest in health and fitness is increasing, offering increased opportunities for graduates who want to provide fitness services, or key into lifestyle choices. There are management opportunities within local authority and privately run health centres as well as freelance opportunities for fitness trainers.

Museums and galleries are also part of the leisure and tourism industry and there's a general push to widen the appeal of these locations and get more visitors through the door. As well as finding new ways to publicize these places, many museums have undergone a process of rethinking and redesigning in order to make the exhibitions they run more interactive. The use of multimedia technology and perhaps more theatrical skills has helped to ensure that the public engage with exhibitions and have an enjoyable as well as a learning experience.

The gaming industry – PCs, consoles and online centres – is a massive and expanding market requiring skills from other disciplines such as IT, media and promotion. With gaming budgets now reaching the level of major film releases, this area of leisure will offer high-flying creative-minded people incredible opportunities for their career, whether they take full-time permanent work or project-by-project short-term jobs.

Ways into the workplace

There are a myriad of levels and roles through which you can enter the tourism and leisure industry. You can get good work experience or enter the industry through summer jobs, both in the UK and abroad, with package tour operators, hotels, campsites, resorts, visitor attractions, restaurants, event companies and local tourism organizations. The UK market in this area is seasonal, so make sure you apply two or three months in advance of summer to ensure that you stand a chance.

As a graduate, all these organizations will be able to offer you management or supervising positions. There may also be opportunities at a more strategic level within local or national tourist boards and within local government where the promotion of an area is regarded as an important task in terms of generating income and therefore boosting the economy of an area. It should be remembered that the Department of Culture, Media and Sport (www.culture.gov.uk) is directly responsible for policy in these areas and funds the work of other leisure bodies, including the Sports Council. You can look for work at the Department itself or use the Web site to keep yourself informed of industry trends.

Leisure centres, fitness centres and sports venues may have opportunities for you to use your professional skills, whether in back-office management, promotions or on the front line interfacing with the public, taking fitness classes or designing and running individual fitness plans and programmes.

The games industry is harder to crack unless you have skills in IT or a high level of games knowledge. However, as the games industry becomes increasingly interactive and gamers become more demanding, there will be more opportunities for people with high-level gaming concepts which can be implemented by companies regardless of whether you know how computer code works.

Indeed, the key to future success in the industry is finding and making links between a variety of disciplines. On a basic level the successful management of a theme park requires interaction between a ride designer, a ride engineer, a marketing professional and a personnel manager – all of whom will ensure that a new ride addresses the demands of the public, fits perfectly into the current surroundings of the theme park and is operated safely and efficiently by park staff. In a similar way, local tourism managers may get involved in matters such as architecture and planning permission to ensure that any development within their area does not compromise the physical attraction of that area for tourists. In both cases, managers and decision makers working on the project must consider each development from a variety of viewpoints to ensure that the maximum positive impact is created.

Professional bodies offering jobs, information and further education

Chartered Institute of Marketing
Moor Hall, Cookham, Maidenhead, Berkshire SL6 9QH;
Tel: 01628 427500; www.cim.co.uk.
Runs and recognizes a range of sector-specific marketing and promotional-based courses.

Tourism Management Institute
Clive Wyatt, Winchester City Council, City Offices, Colebrook Street, Winchester SO23 9LJ; www.tmi.org.uk.
Recognizes and represents professionals in destination management.

Institute of Leisure and Amenities Management (ILAM)
ILAM House, Lower Basildon, Reading, Berkshire RG8 9NE;
Tel: 01491 874800; www.ilam.co.uk.
Publisher of *Leisure Manager* magazine; runs continuous professional development courses.

Institute of Leadership and Management
1 Giltspur Street, London, EC1A 9DD; www.i-l-m.com.
Recognizes courses and qualifications for those in management and supervisory roles.

Institute of Sports and Recreation Management (ISRM)
Gifford House, 36–38 Sherrard Street, Melton Mowbray,
Leicestershire LE13 1XJ; Tel: 01664 565531; www.isrm.co.uk.
Jobs, information and courses.

The Tourism Society
26 Chapter Street, London SW1 4ND; www.tourismsociety.org.
Provides a professional forum for all those concerned with tourism industry; student membership available.

Become a Professional Railway Engineer

Introduction

So you are working your socks off studying for an engineering degree (or have already completed one), and now want to decide how to apply your engineering expertise in a working environment. How about a career in Railway Engineering? You may be surprised to know that the Railway industry can offer significant challenges and a lifetime of interest. Remember, engineers make things happen, and this is especially true in railways where the whole day-to-day railway operation is carried out in an intensely practical engineering environment. Every aspect of this depends upon successful engineering, calling in turn for highly competent engineers.

Train Operators Need You!

Engineering is vital for the delivery of a sound and satisfactory railway service. Railway engineers provide the infrastructure, locomotives, vehicles and physical environment in which to operate. Many companies in the railway industry are seeking to employ engineering graduates. Amongst these are the Train Operating Companies who, between them, run a fleet of over 12,000 passenger carriages and locomotives plus freight fleets across Europe. All of these vehicles must be efficiently maintained and fit for use: engineers take the lead in getting this to happen. Whether working on vehicle design, specification or procurement, with operational and engineering safety or with the risk based maintenance regimes, engineers are involved at every stage of the operation.

On offer ...

Railway companies offer comprehensive training schemes, accredited by the professional engineering institutions. You can expect training to be comprehensive and provide a fast-track route to becoming a Chartered Engineer. You will need to have (or be studying for) a MEng or BEng degree in either Electrical or Mechanical Engineering. This should be accredited by a professional engineering institution. You will also need to have the ability to apply your knowledge in the real world of businesses and people. It can be helpful to have good job mobility for career development because jobs may well arise over a wide range of geographical locations.

RAILWAY ENGINEERING

– Join the Master
RE-CREATE BRITAINS RAILWAYS

Train Operators offer a challenging and stimulating career for ambitious engineering graduates – railways were built by some of the world's greatest pioneering engineers. The same skills, spirit and determination are needed now – to re-create nothing less than the re-birth of Britain's railways.

Our engineers handle a wide range of technical issues. These include engineering design, equipment specification and the definition and management of vehicle maintenance regimes.

On Offer

A development scheme for graduates designed to lead to a career in railway engineering. Successful candidates will receive comprehensive training to equip them for responsible engineering positions in the industry. Vacancies arise across the country and some train operators also offer 1-year work placements to undergraduates.

We require

Graduate engineers with an accredited honours degree in Electrical or Mechanical Engineering, prepared for the challenge of applying their engineering knowledge in an intensely practical working environment.

Graduate trainees 2002

"The railway industry is a highly challenging and rewarding industry for an engineer to work in. The ATOC scheme provides an excellent introduction to this industry and is providing me with the tools and experience that I need to make the most of my career as a railway engineer."

Ian Robinson, Network Rail, Derby

uctured, progressive, responsible professional development."

Grant Lovering, Silverlink Trains, London

"Joining the railway industry has allowed me to work on a variety of different projects with opportunities to travel. The railways offer a secure, expanding and exciting future where the talents of engineers will always be required."

Gareth Houghton, EWS-Railway, Nottingham

For further information and an application pack contact:
Association of Train Operating Companies
40 Bernard Street, London, WC1N 1BY
www.atoc.org/engineering/graduates
graduates@atoc.org

14 Self-employment

Being self-employed means having to provide for yourself all the administration, support and comfort factors which usually come from your employer. This means everything – from sourcing work in the first place and deciding what to do on a daily basis, to looking after your tax issues, determining how much holiday you can take and when you can afford to take it.

There are self-employed people in all sectors of work, extending from skilled manual workers such as plumbers and electricians through to professional, business and creative roles – consultants, accountants, artists, writers and musicians can all be self-employed. Indeed, in some industries self-employment is expected: TV and performance-related media are full of freelance producers, editors and directors who move from job to job completing one project or programme and moving on to the next. In other industries it may simply be one option for organizing your work. If you want a career in PR, for example, you can follow that career by working for a large PR company, a small niche agency, the PR department of a company or on a self-employed basis.

Many people go self-employed following a period of working for a larger organization within their chosen industry. During this time they will have learnt about their profession and the world in which they work. They will have seen how the industry operates, how their own role keys into that operation and what kind of value they can bring to organizations. Most importantly, they will have established many useful contacts throughout the industry. In this way, when they go freelance they will already have work lined up or at least will know whom they need to approach in order to get that work.

You will need to consider where you are going to work – can you dedicate a part of your home to the activity or should you invest in your own office elsewhere? Even if you spend much of your time working at your client's location, you will still need storage space and possibly somewhere to do your administration work at home.

Selling yourself

In many ways, being self-employed is about selling yourself as a business rather than as a person. You need to identify your unique selling points – the work and value customers can only get by using you. You will need to create an image for yourself – which could mean a carefully designed logo, a clear business card or just a good reputation. You need to put yourself into a position where, whenever your customer decides they need a particular job doing, they immediately think of you.

The idea of self-promotion can be enough to send some graduates back to the careers fair in search of a multinational employer in which to hide, but for many others, self-promotion is simply a habit to get into. It's something that is carried out as part of everyday work. At the most extreme you may want to advertise yourself and your services. Make sure that you locate the right places to be seen – the publications viewed by your customers – and make sure that your advertisement is eye catching, professional and convincing. At the other end of the scale, whenever a project ends, be sure to tell your client that you've enjoyed working with them and ask if you can be considered for further work in the future.

Self-promotion can also be done through your own personal Web site or by sending out letters of enquiry to potential customers making them aware of your work. In both cases you need to make sure that your approach and image are professional, reflecting both the industry and your qualifications.

However, the most important aspect of self-promotion and therefore of successful freelancing is networking. The most powerful way you can get work and continue to get work is through personal recommendation. Once you have successfully completed one piece of work, you can use that project as an example of what you can do for future customers. You may be able to get past clients to supply quotes on their experience of working with you, but most importantly you will have a customer out there in the marketplace who could start talking about you and your work to other people.

Network using your friends and family as well. They may not know anyone directly who can use your skills, but they may know someone who knows someone. In many professions there is a general feeling that the work goes to people not on the basis of talent, but because they know someone. This is true, but one of the reasons that the work goes to those people is that being known increases the confidence that people have in you. They conclude that since your name comes up in certain circles, you must know what you are doing. Moreover, people want to work with colleagues with whom they have some kind of connection. If you are working on a project you will feel more nervous using someone who is unknown, has no reputation but says they can deliver. You'd far rather work with someone who's come by recommendation – no matter how tenuous the route by which that recommendation comes and no matter that they may still have next to no experience.

You need to do everything you can to get yourself known and demonstrate your ability. You may need to invest time in creating a portfolio to show potential employers what you can do. If you're trying to set up in PR, you could develop some dummy ad campaigns to show off your skills. If you want to be a management or business consultant, put together a few suggestions for potential clients and use those as a way into an organization rather than waiting to be asked for your suggestions. If you want to write, you need to sit down and write to prove you can do it. No one is going to knock on your door or phone you unless you give them a good reason to do so.

Finances

Managing finances can be a challenge for the self-employed, and you should establish clear processes to handle this aspect, just as any company would. You need to be clear how and when to invoice customers for your work. You need to pay attention to any specific 'order numbers' or third parties who should be informed of your payment. There are trivial bureaucratic oversights which occur in any company, and result in your not getting paid when you expect.

And not getting paid when they expect is the single biggest reason why self-employed people cease business. Managing cash flow can be a big problem – in the early days of your self-employment you will find that you have an awful lot of expenses – design costs, advertising, letters going out, investment in computer equipment – and it is unlikely that you will see any money coming in for some weeks.

Make sure that you are charging an appropriate amount for the work you are doing. If you've done your research you should already know how much you can charge for your work. There may be standard rates and there may be room for manoeuvre if you can convince a client that you offer better services and better value for money. One general way of determining how much you should charge is to take the amount you wish to make each year (eg £20,000) and divide by 1000 (£20). That is approximately the amount of money you need to charge per hour in order to achieve that salary.

Although there is an increasing trend for individuals to fill out their own income tax assessment, most self-employed people will benefit from the services of a qualified chartered accountant (unless, of course, you are already working as a freelance chartered account). Make sure that the accountant you select has knowledge about the sector in which you are operating – indeed he or she should already be dealing with the financial affairs of other people in your business. In this way he or she will be aware of the various financial aspects of your work and be able to deal with your financial affairs effectively and efficiently.

Support structures

As a sole trader, there can also be a tendency for customers to regard you as their friend rather than their business colleague or, more importantly, their supplier. Consequently, you need to make sure that your working relationship and friendship is not exploited by clients who forever promise that your invoice will be paid, but still fail to do so.

Good networking can help in this support as well. This time, you do not need a network among your clients, but among your fellow workers. In all professions you will find representative organizations and even trade unions that can provide support throughout your working life. More importantly, they will provide a way in to meeting and sharing ideas with people in similar circumstances to yourself.

Self-employment can be a lonely business at times, and you may go through periods of doubt when you think the world is out to get you. Discussing these matters within a representative organization will give you reassurance that it is not just you, and may even identify wider issues which you and your fellow workers can unite over and address with your clients. This provides a sense of unity and camaraderie which would usually come from your colleagues in the workplace. There can be a sense of competition in such organizations, but in general the benefits you receive by far outweigh any negative feelings.

Such organizations may also provide another key support function to your self-employment: education. It is a fast-changing world and lone workers can find themselves left behind and consequently obsolete if they do not provide themselves with regular updates and skill development. Your key to success is to be able to provide a professional service at a competitive price – you will not be able to do this if you have no idea what current demand is or where that demand will lead in a few months' time. You need to be aware of developments – in technology or general practice – which may impact on your work. If you can pre-empt such influences, you will remain at the top of your client's telephone list.

Self-employment requires self-discipline – and this is often what determines whether you can or can't work in this way. If you need other people around you, someone to tell you what to do, when to do it by and what will happen if you don't do it, it's unlikely that you will do anything as a self-employed individual. You need to be able to motivate yourself, to sit down and work even when you don't want to and to see every project through to its conclusion, no matter what is on TV. Conversely, you need the discipline to know when to stop working – when you have really done enough for one day – and to recognize that even though you can work all night, doing so isn't really going to improve your product.

It is most likely that you will embark on a self-employed career as a sole trader, but you may wish to go into partnership with someone. If this is the case, make sure that you trust that person absolutely and that you both share the same clear idea of where the business should go and what you both will contribute to the business. Any indecision or disagreement – no matter how trivial – can spell disaster for the company. Clients will be very quick to spot inconsistencies between you and will shy away if they believe that it could damage the work you are doing for them. If you are looking for investment funds for your business the need for a strong united front is even greater.

There are also examples of graduates establishing collectives or co-operatives – business ventures where each member of the collective or co-op shares the risk and work equally. In general, the more people involved in the decision-making process, the more complicated you will find running such an organization. This is not to say it is impossible, but be certain that everyone wants the same thing and signs up to the same business intentions. Hire an experienced business lawyer to draw up and verify your agreement if necessary. It will save a lot of argument and heartache in the long run.

If you are successful, there is the chance that you will need to employ other people on projects or even as full-time workers. Make sure that you understand the full implications of such arrangements – from paying them correctly through to your own health and safety requirements. Employing others immediately gives you significant legal responsibilities which you may well need further help and support to realize and fulfil.

Useful contacts

If you're between 18 and 30 you can get information, help and even financial support from: The Prince's Trust, 18 Park Square East, London NW1 4LH; Tel: 0800 842842; www.princes-trust.org.uk.

You can also get support from your local Business Link: track them down via www.businesslink.org or ring 0845 6009600.

Advice on small businesses, start-ups, regulations and tax issues is available from: www.dti.gov.uk (the Department of Trade and Industry site).

www.inlandrevenue.gov.uk/employers/index.htm
The Inland Revenue's dry but informative site.

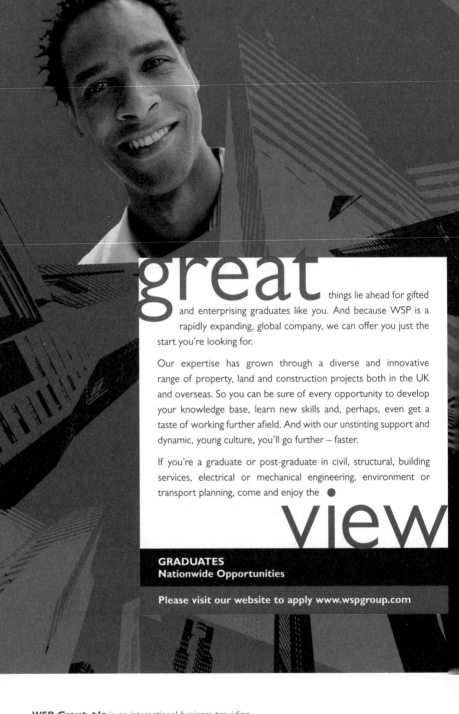

great

things lie ahead for gifted and enterprising graduates like you. And because WSP is a rapidly expanding, global company, we can offer you just the start you're looking for.

Our expertise has grown through a diverse and innovative range of property, land and construction projects both in the UK and overseas. So you can be sure of every opportunity to develop your knowledge base, learn new skills and, perhaps, even get a taste of working further afield. And with our unstinting support and dynamic, young culture, you'll go further — faster.

If you're a graduate or post-graduate in civil, structural, building services, electrical or mechanical engineering, environment or transport planning, come and enjoy the ●

view

GRADUATES
Nationwide Opportunities

Please visit our website to apply www.wspgroup.com

WSP Group plc is an international business providing management and consultancy services to the property, land and construction sectors. We are one of Europe's largest consultants employing 5,000 people worldwide.

www.wspgroup.com

Mhairi MacGregor

BEng Civil Engineering,
Heriot Watt University, 2000

MSc Business Management,
Napier University, 2001

"To be honest, I didn't know too much about WSP when I was considering my options, so I found it really useful to talk directly to someone in the highways section who could appreciate where I was coming from. I was certainly impressed with what I heard, especially about the training. It seemed that WSP really wanted you to get on and achieve chartered status – which of course should be the aim of any self-respecting graduate engineer.

"It wasn't just words, either. I was assigned an experienced engineer who acts as a mentor and has been a tremendous support in setting up the right training opportunities for me. Then there's the work itself. I've tended to work on projects that last about 3-4 months, which is long enough to get your teeth into something, but also allows you to get a breadth of experience under your belt.

"Two projects in particular stick in my mind. The first was the contract preparation for the A34/M4 improvement scheme, which we were awarded by the Highways Agency – I'm now due to go out on site; which is an important part of the process of becoming chartered. The other was working on the design for the new headquarters of the Royal Bank of Scotland. It was good to get some private sector experience and we were also working closely with WSP's structural and environmental engineers – a great example of multi-disciplinary team working.

"I've mentioned two projects, but whatever I've worked on, I've found the people really supportive. Everyone here is approachable and that's been an important factor as I've found my feet. There's a young culture here, it's easy to make friends I tend to go out with people from work in the evening. I don't think you'd find this kind of togetherness in many companies."

ASTON
BUSINESS SCHOOL

BIRMINGHAM

Worldwide respect | we've earned it, now it's your turn

Internationally recognised, highly rated and tailored to the needs of recent graduates, the Aston MSc will stretch you, stimulate you and set you on the path to achieving your career goals.

Visit the school, visit the website at www.abs.aston.ac.uk/pg or for a brochure call **0121 333 5940**

EQUIS

The Aston MSc Taken seriou

Part Three

Or not to work

15 Postgraduate education

Continuing education may be the best option for you if you decide that the subject you have been studying for the past few years still inspires you and you want to find out more. There may be a specialism within the subject you would like to pursue. Continuing education is the worst option for you if you don't know what you want to do so you intend to continue studying in order to buy yourself an additional year or two before making your mind up.

The fact is that you are about to invest more years of your life in education, not only forfeiting time that could be spent making money but incurring further cost to yourself. You might be able to claim some financial support or even a full grant for your course fees but you will still need to cover your own living expenses while studying. If you invest your time studying a subject you are interested in and in which you are likely to find work in the future, then clearly postgraduate study will be a worthwhile investment – the majority of postgraduates find work within a year of completing their study and at a premium income to their single degree counterparts – sometimes attracting an additional £10K or more per year. On the other hand, if you have just dedicated time and money to studying an area in which you are not going to work, then not only will your income earning potential be unaffected (since your employer will see no additional value to the qualification) but you will have greater debts to pay off.

It is worth remembering that postgraduate education does not – and sometimes cannot – follow directly from your degree course. If you want to take an MBA (Masters of Business Administration), for example, you will need to get some experience of working life under your belt. Some postgraduate courses are designed specifically for those who have had work experience, or to complement those currently in work – to provide an academic context and recognition to what that person is doing and learning in the workplace.

Keep an open mind about postgraduate education – when and what will be most useful to your career? Do you need another qualification straight away, or could it be that returning to education in a few years' time will sharpen your idea of what to study and give you a new perspective on your subject? You may discover specific vocational courses later in your career which will significantly increase your earning power – better to wait and find these out than rush into a course with no clear benefit to you. If you find yourself a benevolent employer (or even a half-benevolent employer), they may consider subsidizing or paying for your tuition. Naturally they will only do this because they believe that you will stay in the company and contribute your newly developed skills to their bottom line, but in the long term, additional qualifications will put you in the best position for your next promotion – whether internally or with new employers.

Whenever you decide to take further education, check your course against the following criteria:

1. What value is given to the course by the industry? Is the qualification useful? Will employers pay extra for qualified employees? Is the education establishment well respected or simply an 'also ran' in its field? Do they run the course as a 'me too' offering because every other education establishment offers such a course? Are the tutors well-known specialists in their field?
2. Who has already taken the course? There should be some examples of past students and the successes they have achieved as a result of this course. Do you recognize any of them within your own industry? Can you get in touch with any of them to see how they found the course?
3. What is the practical application of the course? Are there professionally recognized skills you will have as a result of this course? Will you be able to do something which you could not do previously? Will you stand out from your peers with this qualification? What contribution will it make to your overall career?

Standard delivered

Postgraduate education can be carried out through a variety of delivery methods. You don't need to dedicate the next two years of your life to pure study and living on campus, returning to hang out at the student union. You can do your course part time, one day or more a week, or even by distance learning. While this may enable you to integrate learning closer with your working life – indeed, with distance learning you may even be able to hold down your full-time job while studying for your next qualification – remember that the more flexible your postgraduate education is, the longer it will take to get qualified. Hence, a Masters degree done full time could take a year, two years part time or as much as four years via distance learning. It's all a matter of how much face-to-face interaction is expected of students and how much course work needs to be delivered to what deadlines.

These features in turn will be determined by the course you wish to take. Postgraduate education splits neatly down the lines of 'research' and 'course'-based study. As you will no doubt have deduced, a 'research' qualification is a more nebulous pathway based on research which you will need to define for yourself. You should identify an area of your subject that particularly interests you and determine the best way of studying that subject. You need to find an academic institute that would support this research and one or two professors who are knowledgeable of, or at least sympathetic to, your interest.

A 'course' pathway is far more defined. These courses can consist of very particular subjects and modules which you must follow. They are more likely to include formal lectures rather than requiring you to formulate a plan of study with your research tutor. Consequently, course-based postgraduate education is likely to be far more vocationally oriented than research study. There are now diverse Master's qualifications available that specialize in relatively narrow areas of work practice. In an ever-competitive workplace, getting a vocationally focused MA can provide a gateway to future employment – and because of this, getting on to such a course can be as difficult as landing your dream job. The competition is just as fierce.

If you take up postgraduate education following a year or so of work, your education could take you in an entirely different direction to your current career. Perhaps the most obvious example of this is the Common Professional Examination (CPE). This is a one-year course which can take graduates from any discipline into the practice of law. Similarly, a Postgraduate Certificate of Education (PGCE) will qualify any graduate to teach in the classroom, while anyone can gain a TEFL qualification and teach English as a foreign language around the world.

Undoubtedly the most important aspect of postgraduate education is who acts as the awarding body for your qualification. First degrees carry an amount of kudos according to the awarding body – the university attended and so on – but in the world of postgraduate education the stakes are higher. Again, be certain of the value of your qualification in your future workplace before you embark on your study. Ask yourself if this qualification is actually worthwhile, since the proliferation of Masters degrees across every subject means that in some cases you may feel happy to have studied your subject at a higher level, but your future employer may not share the same sense of importance or value of that study.

New postgraduate courses are being offered by education institutions every year and as a prospective student you should make sure that the one you take addresses your interests, gives you vocational skills and is recognized in your workplace.

Studying abroad

You do not need to stay in the UK to further your education. Indeed, in some cases you may feel you must be on a different continent altogether in order to get the skills you require. Perhaps the only institution to run a course that interests you is overseas, or when you think about it, it would be far better to learn a language if you were actually resident in that country. You can even train to teach English as a foreign language in a non-English-speaking location.

Just as foreign travel requires you to find finance to support yourself, you will also need to do some research in order to pay your foreign study fees and to meet living costs. Your search for funds should be centred around the subject you are studying – there could be specific awarding bodies and charitable trusts dedicated to funding international research and learning. You may find that there are sources of funding you can tap into in your country of destination. As a last resort you may consider self-financing your international education. It will be a considerable cost – but, as in the UK university system, you may be able to pick up teaching/lecturing work once established at your college, or other related work to support your lifestyle.

Useful sites and further information

www.studyabroad.com
A US-based information site but with global information.

www.intstudy.com
Another US-based site but with course searches worldwide, advice and information.

www.admissionguru.com
Aims to help students into education regardless of country of origin or destination.

Postgraduates in the UK are not able to access funding through the Student Loans Company. Instead, career development loans are available through the Department for Education and Skills and related high street banks. These are generally between £300 and £8000 but variations exist according to the amount of course fees and length of study period. See www.lifelonglearning.co.uk/cdl/. Tel: 0800 585505.

The Grants Register (Palgrave) – annual publication which includes contact information and details of award-making organizations.

The Directory of Grant Making Trusts (The Charities Aid Foundation) – to be found in most public libraries, detailing grants and awards available.

The Arts and Humanities Research Board – can provide funding for research in these disciplines: The AHRB, Whitefriars, Lewins Mead, Bristol BS1 2AE; Tel: 0117 987 6543; www.ahrb.ac.uk.

www.research-councils.ac.uk
Web site with links to diverse research councils offering funding in different disciplines, including medicine, engineering, economics and natural environment.

The Association of MBAs Loan Scheme will help fund MBA students as long as they have already had two years' work experience. Tel: 0800 200400. www.mba.org.uk.

Some high street banks may run Professional Loan Schemes and Professional Trainee Loan Schemes. Eligibility is determined on an individual basis – including your past record with the bank and their assessment of your income earning potential.

16 Short-term work

Your decision to take short-term work rather than committing to a full-time employer could be based on a number of reasons. Firstly, you might simply not know what you would like to do for a living. There could be a whole host of options open to you, or you may find that nothing particularly inspires you. A short-term job will give you the chance to dip your toe into the world of employment – whether on a general basis or in a specific employment area.

Alternatively, you may want to build up a quick stash of cash in order to go travelling, or simply want to get rid of your student debts as soon as is humanly possible. Rather than taking a set career, starting at a graduate recruit salary, you can maximize your immediate earnings by tracking down the highest-paid job you can do with your qualifications. It may be that one-off contracts and short-term work – possibly with bonuses such as sales commission – actually pay better than the monthly salary.

Short-term work is also a good option if you're developing an idea for your own company or self-employment. You can devote your working life to generating some useful start-up income while also researching the potential for your idea ready for launch. Short-term work will also give you experience of the discipline you need in your own workplace and ensure that your vocational skills do not diminish as you wait for your first customer to arrive.

It could be that this kind of work is a lifestyle choice you want to follow at this point in time. Rather than regarding this work as a stopgap measure between university and your career, you may regard it as the only way to ensure that you always have something interesting to do. You might want to maximize the variety of work you take over your career, and short-term contracts are a great way to experience work in diverse industry sectors.

Finally, depending on your field of work and the economic conditions of your sector and geographic location, short-term work could be your only option for employment. In some areas, the idea of job security has eroded so far that no applicant can expect to work for one employer longer than a few months. The business may simply be unable to guarantee steady work for a longer period of time.

Your search for short-term work can take a wider scope than your search for a permanent job. You can push more speculative letters to a wider variety of employers. If you are only seeking a temporary post, there is more likelihood that employers will be able to find funding to support your work. They may find the idea of using you and losing you more attractive than taking you on full time and then having to be the ones to 'let you go'. If you don't expect job security, it is one less thing for your employer to worry about.

However, while you may feel that you do not need to commit yourself as completely to a short-term employer as you would to a permanent employer, you must always approach and deal with your employer in a professional way. Indeed, there are areas you should be particularly exact about in your dealing to ensure that your employment is beneficial for everyone.

Up front

You can contact your future employer using any of the methods used for contacting permanent employers. Employers at careers fairs may tell you if they are looking for short-term workers as well as permanent staff, but you can always use this initial contact to enquire as to the company's position on short-term work. You can approach companies in writing through letters of enquiry and watch your industry press for stories that suggest that a particular company might be on the lookout for short-term help.

In general, for professionally qualified workers, the short-term work you can secure will demand specific skills and for you to complete a specific part of a project. A computer software company, for example, may be working on a new program or game and therefore require talented programmers to take on specific aspects of that programming. A management consultancy firm could be expanding its operations and want to engage a finance auditor on a short-term basis. Getting a well-paid, short-term job is more of a 'niche marketing' exercise than the general approach required to get a permanent job. Rather than being concerned with you as a well-rounded individual, the short-term employer needs only the reassurance that you are capable in specific areas. They will want to see your job-specific skills, and will be less concerned that your extracurricular activities include being a keen athlete with an interest in ornithology.

Get it in writing

Since you will work on a specific project creating a specific outcome, make sure that both you and your employer understand entirely what is expected from you. The time you spend working here is going to be limited. You need to make clear what precisely is involved in this employment:

● How long is the work for?
● What is the work?
● How will you deliver the work?
● Where will you work?
● How much will you be paid for that work?
● When will you receive payment?
● What are the tax arrangements for this payment?
● What will happen if deadlines are not met – due to your performance or due to unforeseen factors? Will you get more money if it is agreed that the project needs more time to be completed?

If your employer is used to contracting out short-term work or regularly uses skilled employees in this way, some or all of this will be clear from their perspective. However, it is in your interest to make sure that these arrangements are appropriate before you start work. Consider whether you think the deadlines involved are realistic and whether the amount of money you will be paid is worth the job. Be certain you know the rules before you start working – what are your hours and how available do you need to be for your employer?

On completion

Having completed the job, you may decide that this is the kind of work you'd like to do – whether on a permanent or continuing temporary basis. Make sure that you maintain contact with your employer – or at least carry out a debriefing session where you discuss the success of the project, determine that you can use your employer as a reference for future work and that they will call you if similar opportunities arise in the future. On the other hand, you may feel that this work really doesn't suit you. This is still a positive outcome, since you haven't signed up to more years of the same. Study the experience: consider what you liked and disliked about the work – what you did, location, work style, work colleagues – and what aspects were acceptable. You can then move on and find a more satisfying role.

Underemployment

Sometimes graduates find themselves in short-term work that does not take full advantage of their skills and qualifications. These are similar to summer jobs or Saturday jobs they may have had while they were students – or even at school. While not well paid, these kinds of jobs can be a way of making ends meet while waiting for the first 'proper job' to arrive.

If you find yourself in this position, it is important not to let your circumstances discourage you. It is easy to feel that after all that hard work and education you've ended up back where you started, but in reality your situation is better than before and you simply need to be patient for the right opportunity to arise. These kinds of jobs may also be acceptable to you because they are not very demanding – you haven't immediately gone into a high-pressure situation as soon as you finished your high-pressure education. You could find that doing something that uses little energy or brainpower means that you can focus that energy on your own projects outside working hours.

At the same time, you may find that returning to be a shop assistant at the same place you worked before graduating offers a useful way into the company's graduate recruitment scheme. Now that you are qualified and able to demonstrate commitment and an interest in your employer's company, they may regard you as the perfect applicant for future management.

Connect Youth

Giving young people international experiences

Would you like to travel abroad and meet young people from other parts of the world?

Connect Youth offers programmes that give young people an international experience. Every year we send and receive over twenty thousand young people on programmes ranging from group youth exchanges to individual voluntary service. We believe that bringing young people together not only provides them with the opportunity to experience and appreciate new cultures but also teaches them more about themselves.

For groups of young people between 15 and 25 years, we offer funding for:

- *travelling abroad, meeting groups of young people from different countries, taking up activities of mutual interest and host groups from abroad in return*

- *creating, devising and managing projects within the local community. Past projects have covered various themes from youth newspapers to arts festivals and trading enterprises.*

For individual young people we offer:

- *the European Voluntary Service, which allows individual young people aged 18 to 25 to act as volunteers abroad, for a period up to a year. They can work in a variety of settings including the care sector, with children, people with disability, or with the elderly*

- *you could also join summer camps in Israel, the West Bank or Macedonia, and teach English to young children.*

Our programmes are open to all British young people; there are no entry qualifications to take part. You can choose from over forty countries from Europe and beyond. All activities are supported by funding from the European Commission (European YOUTH Programme), Foreign and Commonwealth Office and the Department for Education and Skills.

For more information, contact
Connect Youth
British Council
10 Spring Gardens
London SW1A 2BN
Tel 020 7389 4030, Fax 020 7389 4033
Email connectyouth.enquiries@britishcouncil.org
www.connectyouthinternational.com

17 *Travel the world*

Now is the time to exploit all the special travel offers available to you as a young person. Anything from a rail trip around Europe to a round-the-world flight will be cheaper for you now than ever again. If you're feeling confident about your future career and believe that you will be able to walk into a job on your return, you can throw caution to the wind for the next 18 months or so, stock your bank balance with another loan, prepare to max out your credit cards and take off around the world.

Travelling will be an option for you at any time over the next few years – you do not need to do it as soon as you graduate. You may decide to work for a couple of years just to get your career started and put a few pounds in your bank account before heading off into the wild blue yonder. In this way you can travel with the assurance that when you return you will not be facing the ordeal of finding your first job and trying to clear more debts.

Some large employers now recognize the value of such a world trip among their graduate recruits to such an extent that they will happily give you the time you require to take the trip and hold your job open for you for when you return. They recognize that it is better for them that you come back to their company, bringing the skills and knowledge you had plus those gained during your expedition, rather than to sever all ties and try to find a replacement for you. Indeed, some companies regard this as such an important issue that their benefits and reward packages can include financial 'golden hellos' which you can use to get on the next plane out of the UK.

Travelling the world should not be regarded as an extended holiday, but nor is it purely a fact-finding learning experience. The idea is not to wend your way from luxury hotel to luxury hotel, nor is it to contract malaria as you hack your way through a remote rain forest. Planning is essential, but you need a degree of flexibility. You should expect the odd detour here and there and be ready to regard any setback to your travel – visa problems, no vacancies at the hostel, all your camping equipment stolen – as an opportunity in disguise. In short, you need to be ready to solve travel-related problems whenever and however circumstances dictate. It is this skill above all else that your employers will look for and expect to see in you when you return.

How to plan your trip

Decide what kind of experience you want to have. You may decide to go around the globe, stopping off at as many locations as possible on your way. Your journey may primarily consist of long-haul flights between main destinations. It is possible to buy flexible flight tickets that do not hold you to specific dates for the journey, but do map out your route around the globe. Alternatively, you may want to explore one particular part of the world in greater detail. You may decide that flight plans and economy seats are for wimps and that actually you'd rather buy yourself a Land Rover and see how far you can get driving across continents.

In each case, meticulous research must be carried out from the start. Not only should you consider the cost of your journey, but you need to think about the amount of time you are allowing for yourself in each location and for the journey between each location. You need to think about what visas you might need to enter and exit countries, and be fully aware of any legal documentation you require if you are bringing a vehicle into that country or intending to drive or carry out some other activity in that country. You need to take the necessary immunizations before leaving the UK and make sure that you leave yourself enough time to have those shots before you head for the airport.

You should have some idea of how you are going to live in each destination. You need to research the options, determine the cost and decide whether they need to be booked in advance. If you intend to camp or live out of the van you're driving around in, you need to know if there are local laws restricting where you can stay and for how long. Your research should cover day-to-day existence – where are you going to eat, how are you going to pay for things, how you are going to get more money if you need it and how are you going to communicate with the locals?

You should also consider the people you are leaving behind. While regular contact may be tricky, you need some system for communication with friends and family while you are away. There may be emergencies you need to be aware of or problems you need their help to solve. E-mail now makes it easy for text and pictures to be sent around the world and free Internet-based accounts can be accessed from any wired-up computer anywhere in the world. But of course, you need to be sure you can get access to a computer in your place of destination if you are going to rely on this for your communication line.

Travelling with friends is a good option for sharing the responsibility of researching a trip and sharing the challenges the world throws at you. However, you should make sure that whomever you travel with is a suitable companion. Being able to have a laugh together down the local pub does not mean that you will still get on when you're stranded in the middle of nowhere because your friend can't read the map properly. You could decide to travel some of the way together and then split up, or agree to meet up in Australia at a certain date and take individual routes in order to get there. Alternatively, some world travellers find travelling companions specifically for the trip. Since they meet solely for the purpose of going round the world there is less chance that they will fall out because of a disagreement over something that happened in the dim and distant past.

You need to be sure of how much the trip is going to cost, and always overestimate the expense rather than underestimating. Don't forget to include a contingency fund in the case of emergencies and make sure that you can access this fund no matter where in the world you are.

It is imperative that you get insurance for your trip – wherever you go and for however long you intend to be there. If you do fall ill or have an accident, the medical expenses incurred could easily leave you and your family destitute. Ensure that cover includes any 'dangerous activities' you wish to engage in – scuba diving, bungee jumping, skiing – and that the cover will pay for repatriation, ensuring that you get back to the UK whatever state you are in. There are numerous insurance companies that offer flexible cover for young travellers, so shop around for the best deal. Double-check the full extent of the cover provided by any agreement – including details noted in the small print – before signing and paying.

Back again...

Your final task in planning a trip is to be certain of what you will do and where you will live when you return. If your trip is going to last over a year, there is no point in paying rent for a property just to keep your possessions there. You may find a helpful friend with sufficient loft space for storage. You may find that your parents are happy to look after everything while you're gone. Alternatively, you may need to factor in the additional cost of storage from an independent space-letting company.

You may have a job to return to, but be sure of where you will live – or at least give yourself sufficient time to find somewhere to live when you're back in the country. After a year or so of wandering around other cultures, you may find it difficult to get back into the swing of contemporary UK working life, so allow yourself the maximum time to readjust and sort yourself out.

Make sure that you still have sufficient funds for when you return. Having spent a considerable sum travelling, you will still need to finance daily living, rent and food. If you don't have a job to come home to, you will need to support yourself while looking for work. Having spent a considerable time travelling, you will need time to recover from the experience and being compelled into work because the bank is breathing down your neck is not the best way to end your experience or enter the workplace.

Useful sites

www.gapyear.com
Extensive independent UK-run site covering all aspects of planning and executing your travelling gap year.

www.gap-year.com
Information site run by John Catt Education Ltd.

www.sta.com – extensive travel site for young people. STA also have high street shops in major towns and cities.

www.1stclassadventures.com – great site for travel inspiration and information.

18 *Working abroad*

Essentially there are two ways in which you can work abroad: first, by getting paid to do so, and second, to volunteer.

Both of these options can happen immediately after your graduation, following further study for a vocational qualification (such as Teaching English as a Foreign Language) or following a period of work in the UK. It may be that you decide to take your skills overseas having gained experience in the UK job market, or you may even work for a company in a position that eventually leads to work overseas.

Clearly there are certain skills that will put you at an advantage for overseas work. Speaking a second language and previous experience of a country's culture are useful for any employer. The business world is increasingly operating on a global basis, with companies seeking to explore markets outside their own country of origin. This doesn't just mean finding customers from around the world, but setting up more cost-efficient working relationships with suppliers from around the world. If you have fluency in a foreign language or two, you will be in demand, whatever sector you wish to work in. And even if you're not completely bilingual, a significant cultural awareness of how to do business and operate in another part of the world will still mark you out for employers.

Teaching English

There is a subtle difference between teaching English as a Foreign Language (EFL) and teaching English as a Second Language (ESL). EFL is usually regarded as teaching English to students while they are residents in their own non-English-speaking country. ESL generally means teaching English to non-native students in an English-speaking country.

It is possible to get work teaching students how to communicate in another language without any teaching qualifications at all. In Japan, for example, it is possible to get paid work with business people who simply want to interact with an English speaker to see how they get on and to hone their skills in this way. That said, a qualification will open more doors for you and increase your earning power. It will give you access to a network of opportunities. With the right network and qualifications, you can teach English anywhere in the world. Your training will also give you a clear grounding on how to teach one of the most difficult languages in the world. Rather than leading your students through the maze of the English language through your own intuition, you will fully understand the rules of grammar yourself and can therefore increase the effectiveness of your lessons.

TEFL training can last anything between 4 weeks and 18 months depending on the intensiveness of the course. You should be wary of any institution that offers such a qualification in less time. The chances are that it will not be regarded with much esteem by organizations that run English lessons – plus it may not give you much in the way of practical tutoring. Make sure that, whatever course you do, you receive clear guidance on managing the classroom and planning lessons. Any effective course will include practical experience with a class and provide feedback on your performance in this context.

It goes with the job...

If you find yourself in full-time employment which has potential for working abroad, you may find yourself finally working on an ex-patriot (ex-pat) basis. In this situation, your remuneration and support package will depend on the nature and generosity of your employer. International employers who depend on ex-pats for their operation have developed significant support structures – both financial and social – to ensure that their workers are happy working so far from the UK. A good ex-pat support programme will offer a choice of accommodation – or help you find a suitable place to live. Your employer will help you manage your affairs in the UK and help with the transition process – everything from furniture removal to spousal support if you are married. Once you've arrived in your foreign post, you will be able to join other ex-pat workers and in this way enjoy entertainment and a social life within the ex-pat community.

No pay, all gain

Dropping the idea of gaining remuneration for your work abroad opens doors to a host of other opportunities. Devoting your time and talents to an overseas concern voluntarily can mean taking a post with Voluntary Services Overseas (VSO) or with any of a diverse range of organizations who run conservation or research projects in other countries. Many graduates find this option attractive since they can immerse themselves in the culture of their destination country while contributing positively to the people and the place where they are staying.

VSO recruits graduates between the ages of 21 and 68 in a variety of disciplines. Applicants can approach the organization with specific skills, with the intention of working on specific types of projects, or they may simply offer their time and talents, allowing VSO to suggest projects to which they might contribute.

For some, VSO conjures up images of living in huts with basic facilities, and while this may not always be the case, you should be ready to live without the modern facilities you take for granted at home. Each project requires a commitment of at least two years, and all applicants to the scheme are thoroughly vetted – including securing references from friends and colleagues – to ensure that each individual will be able to cope with working far away from their native country in possibly stressful situations for that length of time.

One further way in which you could work abroad is to find a conservation or natural science research project to which you can devote your time and skills. If your graduate qualification is in the area of geography, geology, biology or a similar subject, you may be aware of ongoing research and work in which you could get involved. Such work may include a survey of plants or wildlife in a certain location. Alternatively, you may be able to make a more direct intervention, such as creating measures to prevent erosion or assessing and addressing damage to natural habitats.

Positions such as these are unlikely to pay any more than subsistence wages but they may lead on to paid positions. If you impress an organization with your skills and commitment they may offer you more work as and when it becomes available. Until this happens, however, you shouldn't expect to make a living out of the money you get. In general, the most you can hope for is expenses to get you to your working location plus a weekly allowance.

But then you shouldn't regard these opportunities as a chance to build up an income – you are there for the experience on offer. Your involvement on such a project will give you a new and enhanced view on the world, giving you the chance to do something positive and discover new skills. Future employers will be impressed by such activities and be looking for the general work and problem-solving skills you will develop as well as the conscientiousness such activities can demonstrate.

If you are unable to locate voluntary projects, there are also a number of organizations that offer access to research programmes for paying members of the public. These organizations rely on participants' fees as much as their hard work in order to carry out conservation work. This expense could rule out your own involvement, but on the other hand you may feel there is a programme that is worth that investment. It could be a feasible alternative to the world trip you were thinking about.

Before you leave

In the end, whether you can work abroad is completely down to you. No matter how much support you get as a company ex-pat or don't get as a voluntary worker, the fact is that some people are adaptable and willing to forgo any sense of roots in the world while others are not happy unless they feel secure and that they belong somewhere. No amount of remuneration or life-changing experience will alter this basic feeling. You need to be certain that you will be happy if you intend to work like this – you cannot risk letting anyone down once you are out there.

However you end up working abroad, if you are paid for your efforts you will need to be sure of the legal side of the arrangement. You may need a work visa for your country of destination and there may be other legal documentation governing your period of stay. There may be special rules that determine whether you are paid in the currency of your country of employment or if you are still a legitimate UK worker with money going into an accessible but UK-based account.

These requirements will differ between employment sectors, the type of work undertaken and even between employers. Some countries actively manage the addition of foreign workers to their economy, encouraging people with specific talents to complement their own workforce and to plug gaps in the employment market. If you gain your work abroad through an organization or employer, these issues will be managed for the main part by their ex-pat support team. However, you still need to make sure that the arrangements made are right for you. If you decide to manage the working arrangements for yourself, you will need to carry out a lot of research and checking to ensure that you can support yourself financially once you have arrived in your country of destination.

Useful sites

www.vso.org.uk; 317 Putney Bridge Road, Putney, London SW15 2PN. There are regional offices as well which can be found via the above addresses.

www.bunac.org
US-based site, closely associated with working on US summer camps but also features opportunities from other parts of the world.

Teach in China Programme – 52 Poland Street, London W1F 7AB; www.councilexchanges.org/work/ticfacts.htm.
Teaching English programme.

The Frontier Club – 58 Manchester Street, Heywood, OL10 1DL; www.work4travel.co.uk.

Membership club which features diverse contacts for working around the world.

www.support4learning.org.uk
Government Web site with portal and list of further resources for working abroad.

19 Managing finances

Unless you go into full-time permanent work it is likely that your financial situation will be a real concern for you. Whether you take short-term work or continue in education, the amount of money coming into your bank account is going to be more of a worry for you than it is for your contemporaries who are working full time. This doesn't mean that you need to dash out and get a job right now, it just means that you need to be sure how you are going to finance your life for the foreseeable future. On the one hand this will give you a sense of confidence in your first days and months as a graduate. At the same time, there may be other people (financial organizations and maybe your family) who want to know what you are going to do about your long-term financial situation.

Recruits into permanent jobs will be looking for a wage that more than covers their living expenses and perhaps starts paying back loans or overdrafts accrued over their student years. You may not be earning enough to start repayments, but you still need sufficient funds to support your current situation. The last thing you want to do is add to your debts with no long-term financial strategy in place – that is, taking on more debts in order to support further education without considering whether you will gain a higher earning potential, or allowing your debts to rise while applying for work that may never pay you enough to get you out of the red. You need to carry out a similar cash-flow calculation to that described previously in this book. You may discover that there's no way you can make your income cover the expenditure you expect to incur over the next year or so, but if this is the case you need to realize this now and work out the extent of the shortfall so that you do not rack up debts uncontrollably.

Credit card bills and overdrafts may just be figures on paper to you, but ultimately, excessive and uncontrolled debts will prevent you from doing what you want to do. You need to manage your finances carefully at this point to ensure that you keep yourself open to the options or career path you'd like to take. This doesn't mean clearing all those debts as soon as possible, but keeping them under control. Without taking stock or considering the situation now, you may happily do what you want to do now and find that next year, when you want to go back to education or go travelling, you have no alternative but to grab the highest-paying job, because your bank is demanding that you pay back your overdraft.

While further education and unemployment will almost certainly mean incurring further debt, you can take short-term work in order to cushion the blow. By taking short-term contracts you are not saddled with a fixed income over the next few years and fixed holidays. You can mix up employment activities, playing off jobs that pay a lot of money against jobs that pay less but are more rewarding. After a period of high-income generation in a sales job, for example, you could take unpaid voluntary work in order to gain valuable experience or skills in another area. Alternatively, you could follow a high-earning period with a swift trip to another part of the world. Doing it this way means that your financial situation could be exactly the same when you get back from your trip as it was when you left university – the point being that your travel has not made an additional dent in your overall finances.

Time to pay

Even if you are able to support your lifestyle and financial responsibilities in the short term, there will come a time when your bank will start frowning on your overdraft or you will realize that the amount of money you pay for the monthly interest on your credit cards is significantly reducing the amount of cash in your pocket.

Whatever your circumstances, you should have some idea of when this will happen. If you are staying in the education system, you should find out what implications this will have on your earning power in the future. What kind of work will you eventually get? How much will this pay? What impact will this have on your ability to clear your debts? If you have taken a relatively low-paid short-term job, are you certain of the value of this post? Will you be able to use your experience here in order to secure a better-paid job or is it simply a stopgap measure that will not key into your overall earning power at all?

There isn't a right or wrong answer to these questions, it is just a matter of being aware of the implications of your choice. You need to be realistic about your financial future and fully aware of the impact that decisions you take now have on the rest of your life. This is not to say that you need to have your entire life path sorted out and defined right now, but you need to make sure that you don't do anything now that negatively impacts on the future. It would be incredibly frustrating, for example, if you were to spend an extra two years in full-time education and end up gaining a qualification that was not valued by any future employer. If you are going to invest time and finance into more education, are you going to be happy if you end up being recruited to the same rung of the career ladder at the same level of remuneration as a single-degree graduate recruit?

Other sources of financial help

You may have the option of taking financial support from friends or members of your family. As you are a recent graduate, they may be sympathetic to your situation and more than keen to help. While extra funding is always useful, be certain as to how this money will be spent.

Your student loan and overdraft are accepted as part and parcel of being a graduate. Personal financial help, however, comes with visible and not so visible strings attached. If you receive money from your parents, what is it for? You may use this money as an investment which will help you establish your business, buy a computer to work from and tide you over before your first customer coughs up. Alternatively, this money might have been given to you to help out while you are searching for work.

Be certain what your creditors are expecting. If you spend all that money and have still done nothing to get a job, whoever gave you that finance could prove more of a thorn in your side than any bank.

At least bank managers will stick to the point of how to manage your finances, but your family could well drag in how much money they've already invested in your education and how you are still dependent on them. Taking the money and giving nothing back is great way of providing them with the ammunition they need to force you into a job you don't want to do. The pressure is on you to demonstrate that you can do something more than 'spend my money on beer' and if you value your family relationships and want to be able to talk to people in the future, don't mix those relationships with money. If you become known as a bottomless pit for financial support you could end up being an outcast – at least until you write a cheque for the money's return that doesn't bounce.

Self-discipline and planning ahead

Not entering full-time employment requires far more self-discipline than agreeing to an employer's terms and conditions. While an employer may make new demands on your talents and time and you may find the whole experience tiring and overwhelming, if you do not take that route then not only do you need to create your own rules, but you need to make sure you stick to them.

The rules you need to set must govern every aspect of your life. If you are not told when to come to work and for how long you should work, then what activity are you going to undertake and for how long? If you are setting up your own business, how long will you devote to that activity every day? If you are taking short-term work, what terms and conditions are you going to be looking for? If you want to go travelling, where will you go, when, and how expensive should the trip be? If you are going back into education, where are you going to study and what will be the subject of your study?

A permanent employer might be able to give you an indication of where your career will go in the future – or at least you will have some idea of your future career according to the sector in which you have chosen to work – but without this apparent structure you will need to set targets for yourself. If you have your heart set on being the managing director of your own large computer consultancy in five years' time, you need to start thinking about how that company is going to be created now. You can't simply set out on your own, take whatever work comes your way and expect the business to land on your doorstep by chance.

It is perfectly legitimate to decide that the next few years will simply be a time of exploration for you. You may not be certain exactly where you want to be in five years' time, but so what? You can still go and try your hand at any number of roles or tasks and find out what you want to do. If this is your situation then you need to be even more determined and disciplined to go out and engage with the world. You need to be ready to apply yourself to a wide range of activities even though they may not be ideal for you.

As a student, there was always the temptation to miss the early lecture, roll over and go back to sleep, safe in the knowledge that you could crib the notes from someone else. In real life there are no notes to crib from. You can't get up at midday, wander down to the kitchen and borrow a job and pay packet from someone else. If you found you were always dragging yourself to lectures and tearing yourself away from the TV to write that essay while at university, it is probably going to be better for you to find an employer as soon as possible who can provide you with the right structure and incentives to get you up and working.

You should not waste the freedom you have by wandering aimlessly around town all day or spending every night out on the town until the small hours simply because you don't have to get up in the morning. Not only will you quickly end up in financial trouble, but you will not be able to operate to your full potential. You need to be responsible about this part of your life. Sure, immediately after you graduate you can reward yourself with some serious fun time, but don't let that extend uncontrolled across the next three or four years.

What you are worth

As a fresh graduate you are attractive to many people. You are regarded as someone with new ideas, a fresh outlook and bags of energy and enthusiasm. Your options are open: you can make the choice between work, further education and travel or anything else that comes to mind. But remember that every year a new mass of graduate recruits like you will enter the workplace. Each time this happens, the competition for graduate appointments gets tougher as you are among an increasing number of graduates searching for that brilliant job. If you sit around doing nothing you will become less and less attractive to any employer. Your degree will become more and more dated and your skills less and less relevant to the workplace.

Your qualification has a value for employers, but as time goes by that value declines. If you decide not to find work which uses that qualification, you may find that the value of your qualification disappears rapidly. Someone with a BA, for example, who goes into an administration post with a local arts organization will be a more attractive candidate to other arts organizations than someone who graduated with the same qualification at the same time but has done nothing in the interim. At the same time, the graduate who went travelling for a year, or staged their own work in a local theatre or got involved with a charity arts scheme might stand a better chance because they can highlight examples of putting into practice the learning they received as a student.

As time goes by, the subject and standard of the degree you have achieved become less and less important to employers. What they expect to see is a good employment history showing impressive projects completed and worthwhile contributions made by you to previous employers. If you are considering postponing your entrance to the world of work you must be sure that your future employers will see this action as a positive or understandable decision to take. They will be worried if there are holes in your employment history for which you do not have a good explanation.

Decision time

Whatever you decide to do – or not to do – in the immediate future, you should be aware of when you need to make important decisions. If you decide to go travelling immediately, should you decide now what work to take when you return or deal with it when you get back? If you take a short-term contract, do you need to know before you start working whether you are happy for this work to extend beyond that initial contract or whether you want to move on once the project is complete? Are you open to a full-time permanent contract with your short-term employer if such an offer were made?

No matter what you decide to do now, there will come a time when you need to deal with the realities of the world. There will be a time when the financial pressures you are under need to be dealt with – when you will need money and when you will need to find gainful employment. With careful planning you can control when this time comes and be ready for it. You can live the next few years of your life in an unstructured and carefree manner but you need to do that in the context of understanding your responsibilities. Unless you are certain about this it is likely that a few years down the line your carefree attitude will come to an abrupt and far from carefree end.

Part Four

Practical advice for the undecided

21 Researching the options

You've just finished – or are about to finish – many years of structured education. While you've been interested in the subjects you've studied, you may not have any idea what you want to do with your knowledge and skills. Indeed, you may not even be fully aware of what you can do with these skills.

Do not panic. There are many people in your situation. To some extent you are in a better situation than those who have already made up their minds what they want to do. While they may head off to the careers fair to sign up to the graduate recruitment scheme for their employer of choice, you can go to the fair, have a look around and see what appeals to you.

If you have a single-minded one-option-only attitude towards your career you may suffer badly if there are unassailable barriers in your way. Get rejected by your employer of choice – and with so many qualified applicants out there it is a likely occurrence – and you may have to reassess your career trajectory completely. Taking a wider, more flexible approach means that you are open to a greater number of opportunities – chances which you may not even be aware of now. Yes, you are going to make a concerted and professional application to those employers who appeal to you, but you will not be devastated if they don't fully appreciate your talents. If they reject you, it demonstrates that there is a better position for you elsewhere with an employer who will understand your skills and be able to offer you far better opportunities. By taking this attitude you will also be sure always to present yourself honestly to employers rather than bending your personality, skills and CV too much to match what you perceive to be the important aspects of what they want.

With your positive and open attitude in place, you can fire up your enthusiasm and inquisitiveness in equal measure and go in search of your career.

Careers fairs

If you're not sure what you want to do, careers fairs are an excellent starting point to find out what opportunities are available. It has been suggested by some that due to sheer numbers of attendants at careers fairs, the likelihood of a graduate securing work through attending such an event is extremely remote. However, these are an ideal opportunity to meet employers, for them to meet you and to see how you all get on. Take your CV and make an effort to look respectable (smart casual) because you never know who might be there and what might take your fancy.

You can treat careers fairs as a chance to go window shopping: don't just visit the employers you expect would be interested in you and your qualification, take a look at the employers who interest you regardless of whether you think they would employ you. No matter what degree you have, there may be a conversion course or induction course that gives you a way into this employment area.

Ask as many questions as you can of the people at the careers fairs. Find out what it's like to work for that company or that industry. How do they perceive the future of the industry? Is the company facing a major challenge in the near future which will have a significant impact on employment there? Don't be afraid of showing your ignorance at these events – if you don't ask you won't know – and everyone loves the opportunity to talk about themselves.

Look out also for special careers fairs. Rather than running an event that covers general opportunities for graduates you may find that there are dedicated sessions for working abroad, working in the voluntary sector and getting work experience. Some of these niche events only occur in larger towns or cities – sometimes only in London – so you may need to do some research to track down a suitable event for your interest and arrange a day out.

Careers centres

Your university careers centre is an excellent place to find out which companies are looking to recruit this year and more generally to hone your application skills. There are countless books, leaflets and Internet sites you can access via your careers centre, and trained staff are on hand to talk to you about your options or to give you advice on specific employers and applications. Even if you feel the opportunities on offer are mundane or just not you, you may find a job description that triggers a thought or find a contact you can use to further your research.

Read all about everything

Strike up a healthy relationship with your local library and scour the pages of the daily press whenever you can for opportunities or just for features about working life in diverse parts of the economy and country. All broadsheet newspapers have special daily sections devoted to different aspects of living and working in the UK, so you can help yourself to a fresh and contemporary insight into work in areas such as the public sector, the computing industry or the practice of law. Do these stories intrigue you? Are these issues something you'd like to engage with or are they a complete turn-off?

Surf the Internet but avoid plugging yourself into job search facilities for as long as possible. These programs will help if you know what you're looking for – and some will automatically inform you of new opportunities as employers make them known – but they can be limiting in terms of the search results they offer. If you limit your search to only one role or one industry you could be missing out on other opportunities. Keep your Internet search varied and open to chance – enter an unlikely profession into www.google.co.uk and see what turns up.

(Un)official mentor

Think of a celebrity or well-known businessperson you admire and research his or her background. Dig out biographies and auto-biographies and find out how these successful people achieved their careers, what they believe the key to their success has been and what projects they were involved in before they hit the big time. You don't need to match their path step by step – indeed, it would be impossible to do so – but they might provide you with additional inspiration.

You may want to develop a one-to-one mentoring or coaching relationship. In these instances you should select someone who is some years ahead of you and in work who can offer independent and informed advice on your career and the options you have. Identifying the right person now may be a challenge if you're not sure what industry you want to work in, but write to anyone and everyone whom you think could offer you advice to get the view from someone inside the workplace. Ask what they would look for in a graduate recruit and what they would do today if they were trying to get a job.

Check the TV listings for work-related documentaries. Even an entertainment show such as *Faking It* – where a person from one profession tries to pass themselves off as an experienced worker in another – can offer insights into a profession or industry which may inspire or discourage you. The programme *Back to the Floor* featured people from senior positions returning to the front line of their opera-tion – and thereby gave a simultaneous insight into both senior-level and shop floor work in their industry. The viewing public never tires of watching what other people do for a living and more programmes of this type will follow. You can now justify your TV habits as research.

Watch and talk

Talk to people who are already in employment. Your university department should have information relating to what people have done after graduating and you may be able to use this link as a way of getting in touch with them. Ask them for advice, opinions or just anecdotes about how they started doing what they're doing, what they did when they left university and how it felt.

Ask anyone these questions whose job intrigues you or who is working in an area you think you might like to work in. People are very happy to give their time and advice like this (it's flattering to be asked) even if the job they do doesn't appear to be world changing, high profile or remarkable. Indeed, the more apparently mundane the job, the more flattered the worker will be to think you're interested in them.

Are you experienced?

Get as much work experience as you possibly can. As a fresh graduate, there are no end of employers who will take you into their offices to make tea and send faxes. You don't need to do anything significant or even constructive, you just need to soak up the atmosphere of the workplace, understand how work is carried out, how people interact with each other and assess whether you could fit into this situation.

While you will immediately benefit from just being there, in some industries work experience is not just essential to employment but is regarded as the only way to get employment. If you like what you see and where you are, you can start working with real enthusiasm which will be noted by those around you. Before you know it you could be indispensable to the organization.

Get out and about

You will not be able to make up your mind about your future by sitting in your bedroom or downing another cup of coffee in front of the TV. You need to get out and talk to people. You need to discuss your options with others – even if your friends are in the same situation as you they can give you an independent view of what your options are and what they think you might be good at.

Government Communications Headquarters (GCHQ), along with MI5 and MI6, forms part of the UK's Intelligence and Security community. Based in Cheltenham, we are a Civil Service Department reporting to the Foreign Secretary. GCHQ has two missions: Signals Intelligence (Sigint) and Information Assurance (IA).

Our Sigint work involves the use of extremely sophisticated technology to gather intelligence from around the globe in compliance with a strict legal framework which complies with the European Convention on Human Rights. The intelligence is used to support Government decision making in the fields of national security, military operations and law enforcement. Our product is at the heart of the struggle against terrorism and the prevention of serious crime. Whether it be keeping track of drugs, weapons of mass destruction, or providing vital military, political and diplomatic intelligence, GCHQ maintains a watching brief on the world to protect interests vital to the wellbeing of the nation.

Our Information Assurance role is carried out by GCHQ's Communications Electronics Security Group (CESG); they help ensure that Government and military communications and information systems are safe from hackers and other threats. They also help those responsible for the UK's critical national infrastructure (power, water, police, communications etc.) keep their networks free from interference and disruption.

In terms of our cutting edge technology and massive computing power, GCHQ is one of the leading organisations in Europe. But it's not just about technology. GCHQ is also a hugely diverse employer, offering excellent career opportunities across a wide range of disciplines, which are advertised openly via the press and our website (www.gchq.gov.uk). The work is fascinating, the organisation is World Class and, although we try to stay out of the headlines, staff working here often contribute to the stories behind them. Very few organisations can offer such satisfying and stimulating careers.

Helping protect British interests overseas,
GCHQ gathers sensitive intelligence from a variety
of sources. How we use it is crucial to national
security, and calls for specialists in IT, Electronics
& Communications, as well as Mathematicians,
Linguists, Information specialists and Fast Track
Management Trainees. Bring us a good degree and
an interest in global issues and we promise you a
career in a class of its own, where you'll help shape
front page headlines. With our individual training
programmes, we could fast-track you to a senior
management role within five years. And with our
unique range of careers, you'll never be short of
intellectual stimulation. Now, how many careers
can boast that kind of satisfaction?

Applicants must be British citizens.

For more information:
Apply online: **www.gchq.gov.uk/recruitment**
Telephone: 01242 232912/3.
Fax: 01242 260108.
Email: recruitment@gchq.gsi.gov.uk

GCHQ values diversity and welcomes applications
from all sections of the community.

GRADUATES
CHELTENHAM

WHERE CAREERS MAKE HEADLINES

22 How to make the best decisions

Never forget that this is your life and no one can make decisions for you. Anything anyone tells you about work and careers – no matter what it is – can only serve as advice and it is up to you to determine whether you think the advice is good or worth acting upon.

Make the best decision for you as you feel right now. There isn't any special secret to life that you've been kept in the dark about. The fact is, no one else is in your position or knows how you feel. If you make a decision based on what someone else says but not on what you believe then you forfeit responsibility for your life. You cannot turn round to someone else and blame them for what you do. There's no point in saying that you hate your job and that you only did it because one of your university tutors thought you'd be really good at it – this may well be true but it will not be his or her fault if the career you end up with does not inspire and excite you, it will be yours. Moreover, if you do end up working at something you don't really enjoy, it is you who will have to find a way out of that career and into a new job.

Consider:

- What will be the consequences of my choice?
- What options do I lose/gain?
- What can I learn from research/other people?
- Do I have to make this choice now?
- Who needs to know my final decision and when?

Playing the scenario out

What will be the consequences of your decision? What further options do you open if you go down this route and do you close off any other options? In some cases your decision may not have the binding consequences you first think. The choice you face may not be as significant as you first thought. By taking this job in administration now, for example, you may not be cutting yourself off from a more creative role in the future. As time goes by and you learn from your experience in the world of work, you may discover that what you consider to be major choices do not actually influence your life as significantly as smaller decisions you made without thinking along the way.

Time and research

If you are faced with a particularly difficult issue, consider how much time you have before you need to make that decision. If you have sufficient time, carry out in-depth research. Look at the problem from as many different angles as possible – think about the implications your decision may have on your personal and private life, on your social life and on your material life. How much do these individual aspects matter to you and is one of these aspects so important that it must determine what you do on this and every other occasion?

Prepare to decide

Be prepared to make decisions about the jobs for which you apply. In some sectors your interviewers will make you an offer of employment on the day of your interview. In the case of teaching, for example, a school will expect an applicant to accept or decline an offer of employment after a day of touring the school and being interviewed. If this is the case in your sector, you must be ready to make such a decision. Make sure you have considered what you need to know in order to make such a decision and that you are ready to give an answer if you are offered the job. Hesitancy or requesting more time to think about it will not impress your potential employer – no matter what your final decision is or how much more consideration has gone into your choice.

Move on

Don't be paralysed by decision making. At the end of the day, life will go on. Career decisions are important but they are not a matter of life and death. You are currently at a stage in life when you can experiment and make mistakes. You can choose to take one job, discover it really doesn't suit you and consequently take a different option entirely. No one will criticize you for trying something out and learning from the experience. They will, however, criticize you for not doing anything or for agonizing over a decision for so long that the opportunity that was open for you disappears. Time passes, life goes on and letting it go on without you is not a good idea.

Fortune favours

Some choices can be so finely balanced that it's impossible to decide one from another. Don't be afraid to let chance intervene. If there are no significant implications tied to one choice or another, be led by your instincts. Careers can be built from luck and chance as much as they can be designed, so leaving some occurrences to the fickle hand of fate may leave you open to more rewarding opportunities than would come your way if you tried to strategically engineer every aspect of your working life.

Follow through

The best decisions you take will be the ones that you follow through on. You cannot make a choice and then follow through half-heartedly. You mustn't make one decision and then spend the next few months or years doubting whether you made the right choice. It is up to you to dedicate yourself to seeing through the consequences of that decision and to make it the right thing for you to have done at that time and in those circumstances.

Employers may be frustrated by your indecision, but there is nothing more damaging to a business, to a team of employees or to you as an individual than continuous doubt. It will destroy your concentration, compromise your effectiveness and give others the impression that you don't know your own mind and don't care. Whenever you make a decision about anything in your life – stick to it. Don't get distracted by the potential opportunities which you may have now closed down – you need to behave as if those other options had never existed. Don't let others undermine your confidence in your decision – even if you find it hard to verbalize or explain why you have done something, as long as you maintain that what you did was right you will ensure that what you did was right.

Towers Perrin, including Tillinghast-Towers Perrin, is a wholly owned equity partnership of senior employees. We are one of the world's largest independent global human resources and actuarial consulting firms, assisting organisations in managing people, performance and risk.

The firm has offices in 23 countries and employs approximately 8,500 people worldwide, including over 1,000 actuaries. We are a multidisciplinary firm and provide a wide range of specialised services to our clients.

Our graduate opportunities for trainee actuaries are within Employee Benefit Services of Towers Perrin and within Financial Services of Tillinghast, which encompasses both life and general insurance.

Employee Benefit Services helps clients manage traditional pension plans, cash balance plans and defined contribution plans, often using innovative approaches that enable clients to strengthen their competitiveness while keeping retirement programs aligned with business objectives.

Financial Services provides actuarial and management consulting to financial services companies and advises other organisations on their self-insurance programs. Tillinghast consultants also work with health sector organisations and provide risk management consulting to organisations of all types.

In June 2002, Tillinghast took the majority stake in Classic Solutions, who are at the forefront of financial modelling software development.

Training & Development
Graduates are given every encouragement to develop their career, both through formal training and by involvement in a wide variety of client assignments. Working closely with experienced actuarial consultants graduates provide support in all aspects of consulting. Whilst working towards qualifying as a Fellow of the Institute or Faculty of Actuaries, our graduates also develop the skills necessary to meet the challenges of a career in actuarial consulting.

Actuarial trainees are encouraged to develop the skills which best suit their particular talents and ambitions. Early responsibility and contact with clients are also encouraged.

Progress can be fast and the career structure of the firm rewards merit and achievement in both personal development and examination success rather than length of service.

To find out more about the graduate opportunities at Towers Perrin and Tillinghast-Towers Perrin, visit our website at **www.towersperrin.com** or **www.tillinghast.com**

Towers Perrin

Tillinghast-Towers Perrin
Towers Perrin

23 Setting goals and priorities

Considering what to do with the rest of your life can be daunting. There are so many things that await you – not just your career – that you may feel unsure as to where you should even start. There's home owning, holidays, families – responsibilities everywhere you look. There's a huge world of possibilities out there and you need to find a way to access those possibilities. As a newly graduated student it's difficult to get an idea of how everything is going to work out – the mere idea of getting a job and having to do that job every single day for the next few years can seem strange and frightening. You stand at the entrance to the next stage of your life – not yet a fully fledged adult, perhaps, but certainly another step away from your youth.

And if it wasn't bad enough that you are perplexed by the choices facing you, your friends and family have expectations of you as well. Your parents may expect you to find a good job and 'settle down'. Your friends might want you to stay living in the same area as them, they may want you to go travelling with them or to join them in their own escapades in the workplace. So what is your motivation here? What do you want to do and why do you need to do it right now? Why should you settle down with a job and a nice house? Why should you start paying money into a pension scheme? Why should you start saving money each month?

Ultimately, the answers to these questions can only be provided by you. It doesn't matter what anyone else thinks you should do or believes you need. If you're going to make choices, you need to set your own goals and make your own priorities. And identifying those doesn't mean asking yourself what kind of job you want, but asking yourself what you want. So, for the moment, forget everything about deciding on your job and think more about who you are. Forget about good employers, bad employers, pay packets and continuous professional development. Instead, think about your life as a whole and ask yourself this: What do you want?

There follow three time scales through which you can decide what to do next. You don't need to address each one, but find one that inspires you and provides a basis for action. The important thing is to keep an open mind and be ready to consider in more depth any aspect that you find appealing.

Immediate

Life is not a spectator sport and even if you are undecided about your long-term future, you can't afford to sit around and wait for something to happen to you. Without taking the initiative, you will have less control over your life and, while something will eventually happen to you, you may not enjoy what happens. (The bailiffs coming round to repossess your TV is a somewhat extreme example but you could find that someone offers you a job because they know you, know you're not working at the moment and you feel you have to take it. And then you find out that you hate the job…).

What do you want to do in the next year to 18 months? The answer to this can be absolutely anything:

● Go on holiday.
● Get another qualification.
● Move house.
● Buy a car.
● Be in a pop group.
● Lounge around and watch TV all day.

There's no restriction to what you can put on this list. No need for your immediate goal to be large, small, medium sized, include people, exclude people, contribute to the good of the nation, contribute to your bank balance or involve foreign travel.

Write down a list of what you want to do. This should be absolutely everything and anything. It can even include doing the washing up at some time today because thinking about mundane and necessary matters will help free your mind to consider other things you want to do.

Once you've finished you can look at the list again and this time think about what you need in order to achieve these desires. Pretty soon you'll begin to see that in order to achieve anything, there is action you should take now. If you want to continue to study you need to find a suitable course which meets your requirements and which will take you on. Go to the library or the Internet and start tracking down suitable education establishments. Even if all you want to do is finish the washing up you need to buy washing-up liquid, and if you have no money to buy the washing-up liquid you'll have to find some kind of job to give you that money!

This process will introduce movement into your life. Rather than sitting there puzzling about what to do you will find yourself inter-acting with the world around you, which immediately produces more challenges and choices for you to take. You have found the ideal course to apply for, but you need to be able to finance another year of study, so now you need to find a job that will produce that finance. It doesn't need to be a challenging or involving job since you can focus on the study that will follow.

Intermediate

If you're still drawing a blank on what to do right now or you really don't care what you do right now, then imagine yourself in 10–15 years' time. Where do you want to be? What do you want in your life?

It may be that you are able to imagine yourself working at this stage. If so, what kind of status do you want to have achieved? Imagine yourself going to work in the morning. Don't think about where you are going but concentrate on what you see yourself doing in order to go to work. Is that really a luxury bathroom in a penthouse apartment? Is it your turn to take the kids on the school run?

You need to identify what aspects of life are important to you – what elements would motivate you and what you would be proud to have achieved – and then use this to inspire your actions in the present day. What can you do now that will help you achieve those things?

If you see yourself as a recognized professional in your field, do you need more qualifications to achieve this? Can you consider working life in a suit, with all the formal business-like details that go with that lifestyle, or do you think you will be working in a less formal atmosphere? Are you your own boss or working for a top-flight employer?

If you believe you will have a family in 10–15 years' time, how will that family be supported? Are you working flexible hours, or knocking yourself out to support your family and seeing them only at weekends and during holidays? Where would you think of living if you were bringing up kids? Is central London really the best place or do you need a job in which you can be fairly flexible geographically?

The important thing to remember about your intermediate considerations is that these do not need to be set in stone. It is increasingly common for graduates to do a range of jobs over their first few years of employment before settling in one organization or sector as they receive promotion. However, 10–15 years into your career you could, if you wanted to, make a radical change to your working life. You may have spent your first 10–15 years rising through the ranks of retail management – you have had three major employers and are now beginning to specialize in logistics, managing the transportation network which delivers supplies across the UK.

While you have found the work rewarding and fulfilling and are now make a good living, there is nothing to stop you from taking your business and employment experience and transferring those skills into an altogether different profession. Perhaps you want to go into marketing or publishing – you may need to take some kind of course to sharpen your skills or introduce you to the profession, but you can make that move.

People make radical changes in their career all the time. Sometimes it is a matter of pure luck – they meet someone or are picked out by someone for a role that they might not have even considered for themselves. But at the same time you can instigate that kind of radical change for yourself. You could even set yourself a target of following one graduate career for the next five years and then purposefully reviewing your position and redirecting your efforts. The great thing about doing it in a few years' time is that you will have greater experience of what life offers, experience of working life in general and perhaps even the financial stability to turn your career around without compromising any of the responsibilities you have accrued to that date.

If you sit around now unable to decide whether to work in logistics or marketing then the chances are you will do neither to your best ability. No matter which career you choose, you will always be distracted by wondering what would have happened if you had taken the other option.

Long term

Here's the big one: What will you consider the peak of your career to be? Are you a managing director? Do you have your own company? Have you retired early, resting on the millions of pounds you made when your company successfully floated on the stock exchange? Do you split your time between London and St Tropez? What sector do you think you're working in and is there charity work involved? You can be as fanciful and as optimistic as you want to be. At this point in your life anything and everything is possible and no one is going to stop you from heading out to achieve your goals.

If you realize that ultimately you want an easy life full of luxury, you know that whatever you do will have to be well remunerated. You now need to think about positions that would attract high levels of remuneration as early as possible in your career and work backwards from that requirement in order to identify your immediate career path.

Career success is not a causal matter – there is an incredible amount of chance and luck to getting to the top of the heap – but if you have a clear idea of where you want to be in 10, 20 or even 40 years' time you need to start putting the work in now to make sure you get there. Successful directors are not plucked from anonymity and handed the reigns of an organization because they just happen to be there at the time. They are the individuals who have gained the necessary experience and qualifications throughout their careers which give them the skills they need to operate at the top level.

Even at this early stage in your career you cannot afford to let the grass grow under your feet. If your ultimate aim is high, you need to start climbing now. The sooner you engage with the world of work, the sooner you will find how your talents work in this situation.

This is not simply true for the business world. In some industries – the media sector springs to mind – being young, ambitious and ready to try anything is far, far better than being old, experienced and versed only in 'the way things should be done'. As a young high-flyer you can have a serious impact on your employer's business which you may not be able to do in 10 years' time. If you get into your industry early and make a big impression, you will find yourself forever in demand. This demand in turn will ensure that employers shower you with the opportunities and training you require to succeed. You may still be able to rise to the level you require through steadily following the graduate trainee plan and ascending the career ladder when you are told it is appropriate, but if you haven't made an impression it will be a slow and steady process.

Naturally, you can still make an impression on the world in your forties and fifties. You can still turn your career around or launch your million-pound idea in the last 10 years before you retire – but you'll find it all a lot harder. Not only might your employers be less receptive to your ideas, but you may feel more cynical about the world of work you operate in. You may have less energy or too many responsibilities to be able to take the necessary chances. If you have followed a standard structured graduate career it may be that you become content with your quiet and rewarding life. As a new graduate recruit, now is the time to start making noise about how great you are and how great you are going to be. Make it impossible for you to be ignored and inspire others to join you on your magnificent journey through life.

These goals and priorities link together. If you want to be unbelievably successful in 20 years' time, you need to start that process now. But also be aware that your priorities are likely to change over the years. You can't expect to know how you will feel about life when you are in your thirties until you are in your thirties. The world will be a vastly different place from how it is now. Set your goals and priorities, but remember to keep them under review. You will find times in your career when you need to make important decisions –

which of these two jobs do you take? Will you move geographically in order to take a better job? Are you willing to work every hour of the day and night in order to outperform the competition, even if this means that you lose all your friends? You will find such decisions easier to take if you have a context in which to operate. And this context has to be the priorities of what you want to get out of life.

24 Where to get further advice

Careers Services

You can find a Careers Service office at your own university or in the nearest town. Locations can also be found via the Connexions site at: www.connexionscard.gov.uk.

There is more careers advice for people in Scotland at www.ceg.org.uk/careers_in_scotland and via the many privately run careers Web sites.

The Department for Education and Skills is at www.dfes.gov.uk and has links to many different work and career options and information resources.

The DfES also runs www.tea-ni.org.uk offering work and careers advice for people in Northern Ireland.

Sector Skills Councils

Intended to replace the National Training Organizations, Sector Skills Councils (SSCs) are still being set up to meet the skills and training needs for employers and employees in the UK workforce. There are already SSCs running in a number of areas, including Cogent for oil and gas extraction, chemical manufacturing and petroleum industries at www.cogent-ssc.com and SkillSmart for the retail sector – www.brc.org.uk/skillsmart/skillsmart.asp.

Find out if your sector is represented or soon to be represented through the Sector Skills Development Agency Web site at www.ssda.org.uk; 3 Callflex Business Park, Golden Smithies Lane, Wath-upon-Dearne, South Yorkshire S63 7ER; Tel: 01709 765444.

www.bbc.co.uk/business/work – BBC site with many resources, including a Job Bank of employee case studies.

www.channel4.com/brilliantcareers – Channel 4 Web site with off-the-wall approach to finding the right job for you, plus case studies and help with CV and interview technique.

www.crac.org.uk – site for the Careers Research and Advisory Centre (CRAC); Sheraton House, Castle Park, Cambridge, CB3 0AX; Tel: 01223 460277. CRAC provide career advice across all age groups and also run the Grad UK programme that aims to give graduates real work experiences as soon as they graduate.

www.careers.lon.ac.uk/links/uclmap.htm – comprehensive online careers library offering links to practically every job-related Web site you might need.

www.prospects.ac.uk – official UK Web site for graduate employment.

www.ukonline.gov.uk – government site providing guides to important life decisions and aspects of living in the UK. Maybe a little simplistic but does offer a context to every stage of life.

http://www.niss.ac.uk/cr/careers/recruit.html – online resource linking to employment/recruitment sites across media in UK and beyond. Managed by EduServ, University of London Computer Centre, 20 Guilford Street, London WC1N 1DZ; Tel: 020 7692 1000.

Newspapers

All the daily broadsheet papers carry advertisements for graduate opportunities. They also have separate sections devoted to areas such as media, technology and business. Many have dedicated sections for graduates and postgraduates as well.

The Telegraph
Appointments Business File – Saturday
Arts and Books – Thursday
Also: Business Monitor, dotcom.telegraph and media news

The Times
Appointments Section One (graduates and management) – Thursday
Appointments Section Two (technology and senior posts) – Thursday
The Times Law – Tuesday

Also: *The Times Education Supplement* and *The Times Higher Education Supplement* – separate weekly publications regarded as the industry papers.

The Guardian
Media – Monday
Education – Tuesday
Society (public sector) – Wednesday
Online (technology) – Thursday
Jobs and Money & Rise (graduate supplement) – Saturday

The Independent
Education – Thursday
Also: media, network (technology) and the arts as separate sections.

All these papers have corresponding appointment and careers-based Web sites for professionals and graduates.

If you want to track down other publications dedicated to your industry sector, try using The *Willings Press Guide* (Waymaker) which comes out annually and is available at the reference section of most libraries. It lists all publications in the UK (there is a separate international volume as well) and readers can look up appropriate publications by cross-referencing through the index (see www. willingspress.com).

A Fast - Track Career option for Graduates

The phrases Secretary of State, Home Secretary or Secretary General are associated with high level and responsibility in a large organisation. However, when people hear the word secretary in ordinary use, they associate it with basic clerical duties, lower pay and conditions.

The two levels are worlds apart. In today's corporate environment the term Chartered Secretary has a very specific meanings and is associated with the former, i.e. high level corporate administration, governance, compliance and management.

The Institute of Chartered Secretaries and Administrators, ICSA, has been established for over 100 years and its qualified members get to the top, very often to Board level. A recent survey showed that they have interesting and rewarding careers with a high level of job satisfaction. There are many example to be found on their website: www.icsa.org.uk

Business today demands multi-disciplined business professionals who understand aspects of law, finance, corporate responsibility and governance, accountability and management.

Private and public companies, public sector employers and not-for-profit organisations pay higher rewards to people who have knowledge and expertise in these fields. Chartered Secretaries have these skills and get excellent employment packages on a par with lawyers, accountants and other Chartered professionals.

ICSA has a graduate route to a Chartered professional business career that offers responsibility, variety and high rewards. Bright graduates determined to succeed in a professional business career are eligible for direct entry to the Professional level of its qualification and the role of Chartered Secretary.

Graduates can become Chartered Secretaries by completing as few as four final qualifying papers, depending upon the Degree held. Qualifying is a comprehensive package that has all that is needed to prepare for the responsibilities of being a Main Board Director and carving out a career where knowledge, commitment and talents are respected and rewarded.

Enterprise Rent-A-Car

Company Overview

Enterprise Rent-A-Car, a £4.6 billion international transportation leader, is one of the largest international car rental companies with more than 5,000 offices in the United Kingdom, Ireland, Germany, Canada and the United States. With European expansion beginning in 1994, Enterprise currently has ten business groups and 200 offices in England, Scotland and Wales; and continues to be one of the UK's fastest growing privately held companies.

Providing exceptional customer service has been the basis of the Enterprise philosophy and culture since its beginnings. We strive to exceed customer expectations, working in an environment that derives from the traditional values of a family-owned business (which Enterprise still is today). We're committed to the insurance replacement and dealer replacement segments of the car hire market; and take pride in the top level of service we provide our customers.

Career Development

Our company's philosophy of employee empowerment, great earning potential and its commitment to having fun are an exciting change of pace and creating quite a stir. Enterprise gives you the opportunity to run a business, hire and manage your own team and gain business training that helps you succeed anywhere. Enterprise promotes from within, so the trainee scheme is a fast track to a great management career.

The Right People

Enterprise is about challenge, pace and solving problems; yet it's also a tight knit culture, where energetic people have a lot of fun taking ownership of their careers. If you are the kind of person who does it all – and often all at once – and you demand a career that offers a full range of responsibilities, that's exactly what you will find at Enterprise.

Start your personal enterprise today!
- Train to run your own business and share in the profits you help create.
- Obtain highly marketable skills and training management, sales and service.
- Rapid promotion based on performance.
- A fun, team-oriented workplace.

To learn more about Enterprise career opportunities or apply online, please visit **www.enterprise.com/careers/uk**

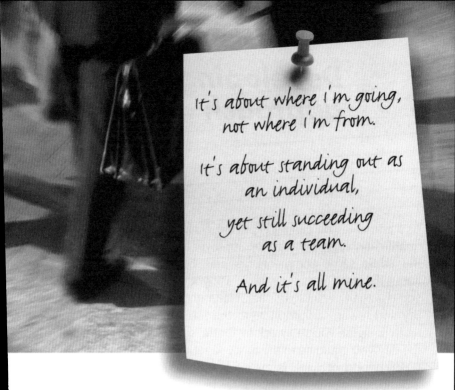

It's about where I'm going, not where I'm from.

It's about standing out as an individual, yet still succeeding as a team.

And it's all mine.

How far I go in my career is truly up to me and my abilities. Sure, every company says that, but at Enterprise, it's actually true. When I produce results, I get promoted, and I've seen incredible earning potential since day one.

Enterprise doesn't expect me to be this great businessperson overnight. They train me. Support me. Reward me when I perform. I'm fast-tracking in a £4.6 billion company with 52,000 people from all walks of life. Yet it's still a tight-knit culture where energetic people take ownership of their careers. And I really enjoy that.

Learn more about Enterprise today, one of the fastest-growing, privately held companies in the U.K. Opportunities are available nationwide. Log on or apply at www.enterprise.com/careers/uk.

25 *Developing a flexible approach*

As a graduate you cannot expect to walk out of university, flash your qualification at your favourite employer and get yourself a job for life. But while some commentators may bemoan this trend and wail about the state of the economy, ask yourself whether, as a graduate, you'd actually want to do that. Naturally we'd all like financial security and rewards appropriate to the job we undertake, but can you really imagine yourself working for the same company non-stop from the day you graduate to the day you retire?

The world of work is an international one. It is easier to travel around the world now than ever before. The Internet and mobile communications have rewritten almost every aspect of contemporary life – from how we arrange meetings to the way we shop, the way we play, the way we receive news, music and the printed medium. It has changed the way we play and communicate. There are more opportunities, more markets, more possibilities in the world of business, commerce and entertainment now than ever before. Do you really want to sign up to a lifelong career which takes no notice of these changes, remains inflexible to new technology but at least makes sure there's some money in your bank account?

There is no question that some companies are using the excuse of a 'poor global economy' to shirk some of their responsibilities towards professional employees. There is no doubt that employers have cut costs wherever they can, removing entitlement to pensions here, scaling down the company car allowance there, and introducing labour (and therefore salary) saving technology. But as that side of the working relationship has been eroded, so too has the amount of loyalty you should have for your employer.

If technology has put employers under pressure it has given employees the chance to fly. With the right skills and the right

outlook you can create a career for yourself which not only provides constant challenge and excitement but delivers high remuneration and rewards. To do this you must have a flexible approach
to your career, from finding and applying for your first job, to
locating new opportunities and ensuring at each step of the way that
what you are doing for a living is satisfying and giving you what you
want.

One approach to this is the idea of the portfolio career. Here,
rather than following a linear career path where you steadily gain
responsibilities as you progress, the portfolio career enables you to
dart around the careers market, strategically picking up skills and
experience as you go. You need not limit yourself to one discipline or
one industry sector. For example, if your ultimate objective is to run
your own PR agency, you might start by learning about newspaper
and reporting work by working for a local paper, then move to the
media relations department of a company, then take a position
outside the industry such as line management within a manufacturing
company – thereby gaining people management and business skills –
before establishing your company.

But you don't need to address your career in such a structured way.
In the next few years you can essentially do whatever you want to do
and you should try to maximize this freedom. You may have debts
but they are nothing compared to the financial responsibilities you
will have when you start a family. You may not like the geographical
area you have been living in – fine, you can move because no one
else is tying you to a location.

You can be flexible in many ways:

- Where you work – is there only one particular sector that will
  look at your qualification and skills? Highly unlikely. Think about
  how transferable your skills are.
- How you work – be flexible in hours. Do you need a nine-to-five
  job? Can you get by on a wage from a three-day week?
- What you do – are you a born leader or do you work best on your
  own? Reassess why you believe you can't be a leader and try
  putting yourself in positions you would usually avoid.
- How you are rewarded – is it imperative that you receive a
  company car and commission? Does the work reward you in

other ways – through doing good for other people or the reward of resolving difficult issues?

● What your prospects are – do you want your employer to map out a career path for you, to set expectations that you must fulfil? Would you rather take control of your destiny, set your own life targets and build your own promotion ladder?

Being flexible means being open to chance. Take a balanced approach – yes, you can have a basic structure and plan for getting your first job and beyond, but if that plan doesn't work out it is not going to be the end of your career. You will not regard what you end up doing instead of that as a failure – indeed, the likelihood is that the position in which you find yourself is better than the position you hoped for, offering greater recognition and use of your talents or providing you with more of a challenge than your original career idea.

Always remember, this is your career and no one else's. As such, the only person in control should be you. Experiment and experience. Don't get stuck in a rut or lumbered with a single point of view. And above all: enjoy.

Index

Index of advertisers